Going Pro with Ableton™ Live

G.W. Childs IV

Cengage Learning PTR

CENGAGE
Learning®

Professional • Technical • Reference

Australia • Brazil • Japan • Korea • Mexico • Singapore • Spain • United Kingdom • United States

CENGAGE
Learning·
Professional · Technical · Reference

Going Pro with Ableton™ Live
G.W. Childs IV

Publisher and General Manager, Cengage Learning PTR: Stacy L. Hiquet

Associate Director of Marketing: Sarah Panella

Manager of Editorial Services: Heather Talbot

Senior Marketing Manager: Mark Hughes

Acquisitions Editor: Orren Merton

Project/Copy Editor: Cathleen D. Small

Technical Reviewer: Jon Margulies

Interior Layout Tech: MPS Limited

Cover Designer: Mike Tanamachi

Indexer: Kelly Talbot Editing Services

Proofreader: Kezia Endsley

For product information and technology assistance, contact us at
Cengage Learning Customer & Sales Support, 1-800-354-9706
For permission to use material from this text or product,
submit all requests online at **cengage.com/permissions**
Further permissions questions can be emailed to
permissionrequest@cengage.com

Ableton is a trademark of Ableton AG. All other trademarks are the property of their respective owners.

All images © Cengage Learning unless otherwise noted.

Library of Congress Control Number: 2012948822

ISBN-13: 978-1-4354-6038-6

ISBN-10: 1-4354-6038-3

Cengage Learning PTR

20 Channel Center Street

Boston, MA 02210

USA

Cengage Learning is a leading provider of customized learning solutions with office locations around the globe, including Singapore, the United Kingdom, Australia, Mexico, Brazil, and Japan. Locate your local office at: **international.cengage.com/region**

Cengage Learning products are represented in Canada by Nelson Education, Ltd.

For your lifelong learning solutions, visit **cengageptr.com**

Visit our corporate website at **cengage.com**

Printed in the United States of America
1 2 3 4 5 6 7 15 14 13

Thanks to Pamela Moncrief. This book took more than a year to write. You made the year so much more special.

Acknowledgments

A big thanks to God for allowing me to write another book.

Thanks also to Cengage for believing in me and giving me the opportunity to write more.

Thanks to Orren Merton for keeping me grounded and focused on my titles and for always being supportive. Thanks to Cathleen Small for always keeping it upbeat and fun!

Thanks to Jon Margulies for taking time out of your schedule to look over my book and keep me straight. Thanks for your suggestions and attention to detail.

Thank you to Dennis DeSantis with Ableton. Keeping us informed and in software has really helped us get a good book together.

Thanks to Bill and Suzanne Childs for continually supporting me when things are good and bad!

Thanks to Pamela Moncrief for your companionship and keeping me in smiles.

Thanks to Allison, Tommy, Haley, and Lexi Parchman. Thanks to Alex, Jen, Will, and Elizabeth Childs.

Thanks to Avoca Coffee (Garald LaRue and Jimmy Story) for giving me a nice place to work when home just isn't cutting it.

Thanks to all the guys at the Usual: Juan, Jose, Louis, Brad, Hampton, Josh, Jordan, Braeden, Evan, and Steve. It's nice to be able to get away from it all in the middle of the night.

Thanks to Livid Instruments: Your products make Ableton even more fun!

Finally, thanks to Ableton for such a wonderful product!

About the Author

Starting off as a small boy on a farm in a galaxy far away, **G.W. Childs** dreamed of sound and music. As he grew, he learned synthesis, sound design, songwriting, and remixing. As a soldier in psychological operations, G.W. learned ways to use sound creatively. As a touring musician performing with the likes of Soil & Eclipse, Deathline Int'l, and Razed in Black, he learned to bring music to the masses.

Still listening to his inner child, G.W. decided to work in video games as well and really stepped into a galaxy far, far away, doing sound design on *Star Wars: Knights of the Old Republic II: The Sith Lords*, acting in *Star Wars: Battlefront*, and composing music for MTV's *I Woo You*.

But the call of synthesis never fully left his ears, so G.W. did a lot of sound design on the popular music applications Reason 3 and Reason 4, as well as the amazing plug-in from Cakewalk: Rapture.

Excited to share knowledge from these wonderful adventures, he has written books such as *Creating Music and Sound for Games, Using Reason Onstage: Skill Pack*, and *Making Music with Mobile Devices*, as well as many highly acclaimed articles and video tutorials with macProVideo and Ask.com.

Contents

Introduction

What started as a simple loop application has become something that defies explanation. Sure, Ableton is a DAW, but it still holds onto its loop roots. It also holds onto its remix roots and includes video—you can use Max/MSP with it as well.

All in all, Ableton is unlike any other application out there, period.

If you add in the fact that with regard to audio, its warping abilities are more seamless than those of any application out there, and then tally up all of these very general features, you have yourself one amazing, underrated DAW.

If you've picked up this book, you have already heard from band mates, colleagues, fellow enthusiasts, and more that Ableton Live is amazing. You don't really need me to tell you this.

What you *do* need me to tell you is that:

▷ This book is designed for a pro user, like you, to get up and running quickly.
▷ This book gives you broken down, step-by-step walkthroughs for the main procedures any pro would want to know, in terms of getting your project going with Live.
▷ This book was written by an old studio hand, just like you.

In writing this, I'm not naive enough to think that you necessarily intend to use Ableton as your main audio app. You may want it as a ReWire slave, you may want it simply to assist a client that uses Ableton as his main app, or you may even be checking it out for live performance, not necessarily as what you use for production. I've taken all of this into account. That's why you won't find long explanations about every plug-in or every little detail about the GUI. This book is designed to get you up and running fast.

In the Contents, you'll notice that everything is broken down by task. And in every chapter, you'll find the procedures broken down even further. With this in mind, don't feel compelled to read the book all the way through. Use what you need, put it down, and then pick it up later when you have more questions. This is meant as a very, very easy guide in "pro speak!"

Also, another thing to consider: If you're an artist who intends to work with a producer at some point in the near future, and you know that this particular producer doesn't use Ableton Live, you'll want to bring this book! Producers, engineers, and so on will always have certain requirements when they start a project. This book will lay out in simple, quick terms what they need—things like MIDI sync, ReWire features/suggestions, export procedures, and more.

So, again, jump around as you need to. Explore the features you never knew about, and have fun. Ableton is amazing, as you will soon discover.

Companion Website Downloads

You may download the companion website files from www.cengageptr.com/downloads.

Setup

C ONGRATULATIONS ON ACQUIRING ABLETON LIVE. Most likely, you're wondering what all the hoopla is about, and you've decided to get your feet wet. And, if you're coming from a background of working with other audio applications, such as Cubase, Pro Tools, Logic Pro, SONAR, and so on, you're in the right place. This book assumes that you have a degree of knowledge about working with pro audio applications and is designed to assist you in your transition to Ableton Live.

This book, which is a part of a greater *Going Pro* series of books, is made up of several tutorials that will walk you through simple step-by-step procedures. If you feel you don't need a particular tutorial, feel free to move ahead to later tutorials that pertain to where you are currently with Ableton.

In this chapter, we'll focus on setting up Ableton so that your transition to using it is smooth and you can maintain your excitement. In my experience, Ableton has always been extremely easy to set up. But there are a few things you can do at the beginning to fine-tune the environment, so that it accommodates your workflow.

Verify Your Authorization

One thing I'd highly suggest at the very beginning is verifying that you have authorized Ableton from Ableton.com. If you don't do so, you're running in a 15-day trial mode, which is fully unlocked. But in 15 days, you'll have a slimmed-down, almost nonfunctional Ableton to contend with. Let's avoid this, shall we?

To check your authorization:

 1. Go to Live > Preferences (see Figure 1.1).

Figure 1.1 Choosing the Preferences option from the Live menu.
Source: Ableton AG

2. Choose the Licenses/Maintenance tab, as shown in Figure 1.2.

Figure 1.2 Selecting the Licenses/Maintenance tab from the sidebar in the Preferences screen.
Source: Ableton AG

At the very top of this page, it should state "Live 9... Authorized" in some form, as shown in Figure 1.3. If it says something along the lines of demo, proceed to the next step. If you're shown as authorized, move on to the "Setting Up Your Audio Interface" section.

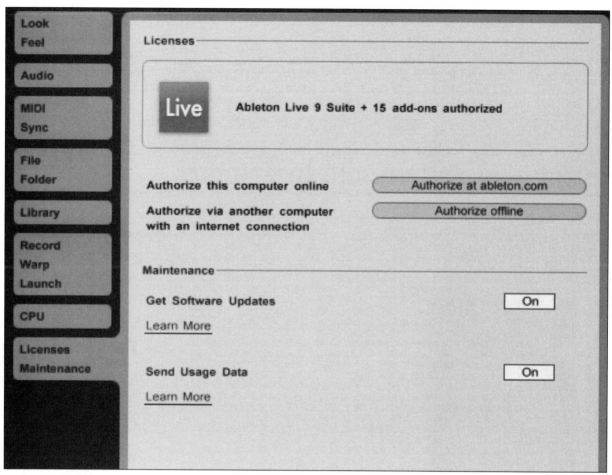

Figure 1.3 Ableton will reference whether you are authorized.
Source: Ableton AG

3. If, at the top of the Licenses/Maintenance tab, it says you are in some form of demo mode, click the Authorize at Ableton.com button, as shown in Figure 1.4. From here, you'll need to create an Ableton account (if you haven't already), log in, and then enter the serial number that came in the box. If you bought Live online, it should already be authorized. You may need to check the email that was sent to you with your receipt.

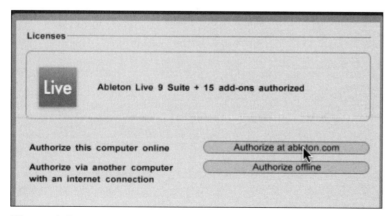

Figure 1.4 Click the Authorize button.
Source: Ableton AG

> **MULTIPLE INSTALLS:** It's important to note that you can, by default, have Ableton installed on two computers at once. If for some reason you need more than two installations, you'll need to get hold of Ableton support. Also, if you've recently gotten rid of a computer and one of your authorizations was used on that machine, you may want to get hold of Ableton support so that they can free up your authorization.

Okay, now that authorization is complete, let's get on to setting up the audio interface.

Setting Up Your Audio Interface

It's critical that you get your audio interface set up, as you well know. Ableton is pretty straightforward when it comes to audio interface settings. But in some ways it's so simple that it's confusing. Let's walk through it together.

1. In the Preferences section of Ableton, click the Audio tab, as shown in Figure 1.5.

Figure 1.5 Choose the Audio tab in the Preferences.
Source: Ableton AG

2. Beginning at the very top, choose your Driver Type, as shown in Figure 1.6. This varies from PC to Mac. If you're using a PC, you'll need to go with the ASIO driver that pertains to your audio device. If you do not have an ASIO driver for your audio device, see the note on ASIO4ALL. If you're using a Mac, you'll want to go with the CoreAudio driver.

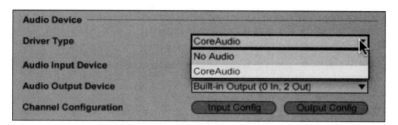

Figure 1.6 The Driver Type drop-down menu.
Source: Ableton AG

ASIO4ALL: If you currently do not have an audio device that has an ASIO driver, I recommend ASIO4ALL, which can act as a blanket ASIO driver. The main function of an ASIO driver for an audio device is to preserve latency, so that you're not recording guitar, vocal parts, and any other recorded audio file that is several milliseconds behind the intended time. ASIO4ALL can help an internal audio device, such as the type found on a laptop. But, it will preserve latency at the expense of your processor.

3. Once you've selected your Driver Type, you'll need to select the Audio Input and Output Devices. Keep in mind that you can select a different audio input device from the audio output device. But in most cases, you should choose the input and output of the audio interface that you're currently using. For example: MOTU Traveler Input, MOTU Traveler Output. See Figure 1.7.

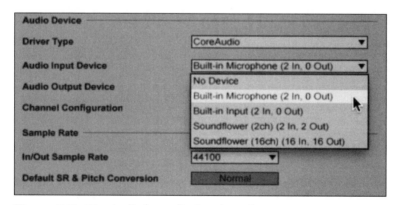

Figure 1.7 The Audio Input Device drop-down menu.
Source: Ableton AG

4. Next up are the Channel Configuration menus, which can be accessed by clicking the Input and Output Config buttons. These menus allow you to enable your audio device's multiple inputs and outputs with stereo, mono, or both configurations. See Figure 1.8.

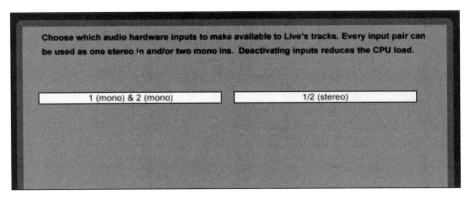

Figure 1.8 The Input Config menu.
Source: Ableton AG

CHANNEL CONFIG: It's important to note that the choices you make in the Channel Config menus will later display in the input and output drop-down menus for individual audio channels in Ableton Live. So, you may want to pay attention to what you enable as mono or stereo. This can be really important if you always have an external synthesizer going into Inputs 1 and 2 on your audio interface; you may want to just keep Channels 1 and 2 as a stereo pair, as opposed to stereo and mono inputs. It just keeps things a little tidier later on, when you're in the midst of production. Don't get me wrong; you can enable mono channels individually, as well as the stereo grouped versions of your inputs. It just makes the audio drop-down menus much bigger because extra inputs are added, individually and grouped.

5. Now that you have the audio device selected, select the desired sample rate for your sessions. Below the Audio Device section of the Audio pane in the Live preferences, you'll notice the Sample Rate section. Within this section is the In/Out Sample Rate drop-down menu (shown in Figure 1.9), which affects the recording sample rate of your current project. Select from:

  ▷ 44100 (CD quality)
  ▷ 48000
  ▷ 96000

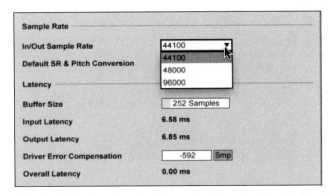

Figure 1.9 The Sample Rate selections for Live in the Preferences menu.
Source: Ableton AG

6. Directly below the In/Out Sample Rate drop-down menu is the Default SR & Pitch Conversion toggle (see Figure 1.10). When set to High Quality mode, all clips will be set to Hi-Q mode. This is a high-quality sample interpolation feature that causes Live to incorporate an algorithm that reduces distortion for pitch-shifted clips at the expense of processor. If pitch-shifted audio doesn't sound right to you, you may want to investigate the Hi-Q toggle on an individual clip or set the Default SR & Pitch Conversion to High Quality for a session and see how it runs for you.

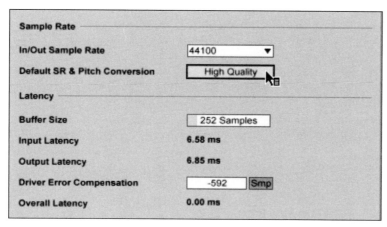

Figure 1.10 Enabling High Quality mode for Default SR & Pitch Conversion.
Source: Ableton AG

Now we're moving into an area of Live that can easily cause a little bit of confusion. But don't worry, we'll go through this together and ensure that your session is tight before you even begin recording and arranging, as only good latency can.

7. Under the Latency subsection of the Audio page of Live Preferences, select the Buffer Size that best suits your workflow and computer processor speed. In terms of latency, this is the most important setting that you'll make up front with Live. Unlike other DAWs, Live does not have default numbers for you to choose from in a menu, such as 256, 512, 1024, and so on. Instead, you can scroll or type in any number you choose between 14 and 2048 samples. If you're unsure of what to select here, I'd recommend typing in **256**. This is a decent buffer-size setting, without getting into the science of it all, and you can always go back and change it later. See Figure 1.11.

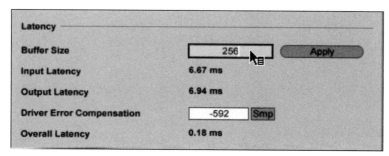

Figure 1.11 Typing in a buffer size of 256 for Live.
Source: Ableton AG

8. After you've entered a buffer size and you've clicked the Apply button, you'll notice that Live will tell you the actual input and output latency according to what it's reading from your audio device. You'll notice that I still

have an input and output latency at 6 milliseconds, as shown in Figure 1.12. Lowering the latency will, of course, reduce the output and input latency. You know that this puts some strain on the processor.

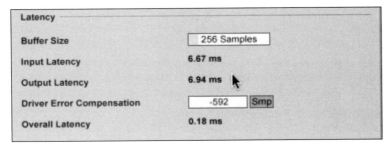

Figure 1.12 Live reporting my current latency.
Source: Ableton AG

Now that you've got your audio device set up, the next step is getting your MIDI up and running!

Setting Up Your MIDI Controller

Compared to many other DAWs, Live is alarmingly simple. Seriously, you almost start looking for more buttons to push just because it almost appears too simple.

Let's start off by setting up a conventional MIDI controller for basic MIDI input.

1. Go to the MIDI/Sync tab in the Ableton Live Preferences (see Figure 1.13). This is the area where you set up your MIDI controllers, in terms of keyboards, to control Live. It's also where you send MIDI sync from Ableton to external hardware—for example, syncing an MPC to Ableton's host clock.

Figure 1.13 Selecting the MIDI/Sync tab in Ableton Live.
Source: Ableton AG

2. In the middle of the MIDI/Sync page, there is a list of several MIDI inputs and outputs. In fact, you'll notice that they are labeled Input and Output before the actual MIDI input or output title. Corresponding to each input and output are Track, Sync, and Remote On and Off buttons. See Figure 1.14.

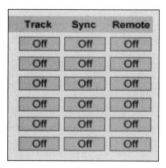

Figure 1.14 Track, Sync, and Remote buttons.
Source: Ableton AG

3. For basic MIDI input, all you need to enable is the Track On. This will cause the selected MIDI input to have immediate control over any MIDI track you create, by default. Before you create a MIDI track, though, I suggest you simply press a key on your MIDI controller and verify that there is MIDI activity with the MIDI input indicator. See Figure 1.15. As you press your MIDI controller, you should see the MIDI indicator light up green with each key pressed.

Figure 1.15 The MIDI input indicator.
Source: Ableton AG

> **MIDI INPUT SELECTION FOR MIDI TRACKS:** When you enable a MIDI input in the MIDI/Sync page of Preferences, you also make the MIDI input available in the MIDI Input drop-down menu on each and every MIDI track you make. So if you're not seeing a MIDI input that should be there, return to Preferences!

4. Select Track On for every MIDI input that you intend to use within Ableton Live (see Figure 1.16).

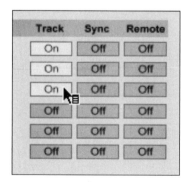

Figure 1.16 The MIDI input indicator.
Source: Ableton AG

Setting Up a MIDI Control Surface

You may also wish to use one or more MIDI control surfaces, such as the Launchpad, APC40, Code, and so on. Or, you may have a MIDI controller that, aside from having keyboard keys, also has knobs, sliders, and buttons. Keep in mind that there are several variations of MIDI controllers on the market, and this section is more of a general setup guide for controllers. There will most likely be some additional instructions from each individual controller's manufacturer.

1. In the MIDI/Sync page of Preferences, at the top of the page, select your controller from the farthest left drop-down menu, labeled Control Surface (see Figure 1.17).

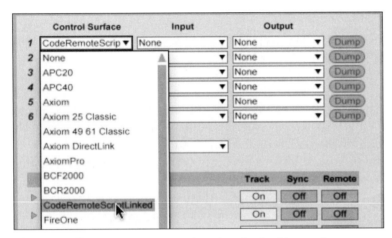

Figure 1.17 Selecting a control surface in the Live preferences.
Source: Ableton AG

2. Choose the MIDI Input for the control surface (see Figure 1.18). In most cases, you'll have two inputs per MIDI device. Generally speaking, it's always the first input. However, if you're not sure or your control surface is one of the more complex devices on the market, make sure you consult the device's installation instructions.

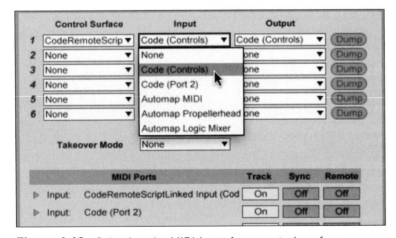

Figure 1.18 Selecting the MIDI Input for a control surface.
Source: Ableton AG

3. Choose the MIDI Output for your control surface (see Figure 1.19). Usually, this is the same selection as the MIDI Input. See the manual for your MIDI control surface if you're not sure.

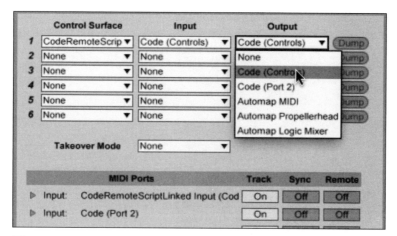

Figure 1.19 Selecting the MIDI Output for a control surface.
Source: Ableton AG

4. At this point, your controller should be set up. Close Preferences and try triggering the device. If there are any problems or something seems off, consult the manufacturer's setup guide. You can also refer to the manufacturer's website. Many manufacturers are really good about posting walkthroughs for setting up certain devices unique to specific DAWs. Because Ableton is pretty popular and so controller friendly, there's almost always a guide specific to Live.

Changing Live's Visual Appearance

Believe it or not, Live has been designed to be slightly modifiable in its visual appearance. For most producers, this may seem like a silly suggestion, but hear me out. Everybody has a different pair of eyes, and some eyes definitely work differently from others. For example, some people can't see certain colors and some people don't like particularly bright colors. Some people just like to match the look of their software to the look of the studio surrounding. Whatever the case, you can actually modify Live's color scheme. If this sounds appealing, you can give it a go by following the steps below.

1. Click on the Look/Feel panel in the Ableton Preferences. This page has various adjustments, including changing the language shown in the Live menus and GUI. There are also adjustments for warnings, labels, and so on. You can even set up rules for what colors clips will appear.

2. Under the Colors heading, locate the Skin drop-down menu (see Figure 1.20). Skins are different color schemes for the Live user interface. Try changing to a different skin—choose Frost.

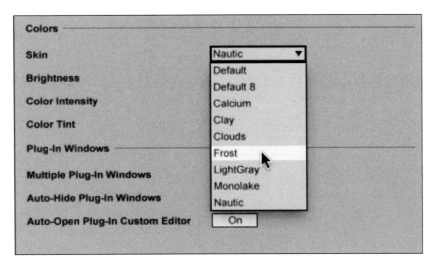

Figure 1.20 Changing Live's color scheme with the Skin setting.
Source: Ableton AG

3. The Frost skin, as you've probably already noticed, is much brighter and cleaner. Even though it changes only the color scheme, it really changes the feel of Live. Now, in the same drop-down menu, change the skin to Nautic.
4. Nautic, you'll notice, is slightly darker than Frost. It's more similar to the other Ableton skins. You'll be pleased to know that you can modify this skin further by adjusting the Brightness, Color Intensity, and Color Tint, as shown in Figure 1.21. Try adjusting these settings until you get an Ableton environment that you feel comfortable with.

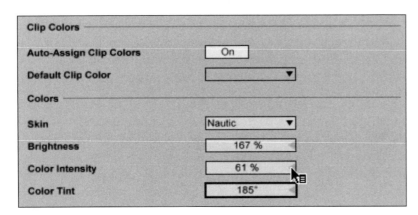

Figure 1.21 Adjusting the Color Intensity.
Source: Ableton AG

Color changes can have a dramatic effect on your creativity. Choosing colors that suit your workflow and aesthetic sensibilities can only help your creative workflow.

Setting Up VST/AU Plug-Ins

Like most DAWs, Ableton supports third-party VST and AU plug-ins. However, note that AU plug-ins are available only for Mac users. If some of your plug-ins don't show up or you'd like to point Ableton to a second VST folder, you have options—take a look.

1. Click on the File/Folder panel of the Live preferences (not shown). This particular page is helpful for changing the location of your temporary folder (where Live places your audio until you save your project), where you can set up your template, and so on. We'll get to these other important setup steps later in this chapter. For the moment, let's continue on with ensuring that your instruments are up and running.

2. Locate the Plug-In Sources section of the File/Folder page, shown in Figure 1.22. This section contains a few options that you'll want to know about. Rescan, for instance, forces Ableton to go through all of your plug-ins again. This is especially handy if you've installed a plug-in while Live is running. Simply click the Rescan button, and Live will re-detect all of your plug-ins, including new ones. No need to restart.

Figure 1.22 The Plug-In Sources section and the Rescan button.
Source: Ableton AG

3. In the Plug-In Sources section, you can also determine whether you'd like to use AU or VST plug-ins at all. If you're running on a PC and you have multiple VSTs installed already on your computer, you may want to take a look at the VST Plug-In Custom Folder function (see Figure 1.23) if your VSTs aren't showing up. Because different companies can sometimes install in different locations, you may want to use this option to point Ableton to the correct location of your VSTs. See your VST's documentation for where it installs by default. And, reference the Ableton manual for setting up VSTs on a PC.

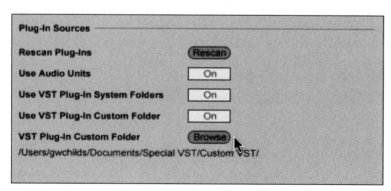

Figure 1.23 Use the VST Plug-In Custom Folder function to locate missing VSTs if they aren't appearing in Live's Browser.
Source: Ableton AG

4. To ensure that all VSTs are available, close out of the Preferences and go to the Live Browser on the left. Look under Plug-Ins. You may have to drag the Browser out to see the selection area fully. See Figure 1.24. If you're on a PC, you'll see only the VST folder. Open the folder and ensure that all of your plug-ins are there.

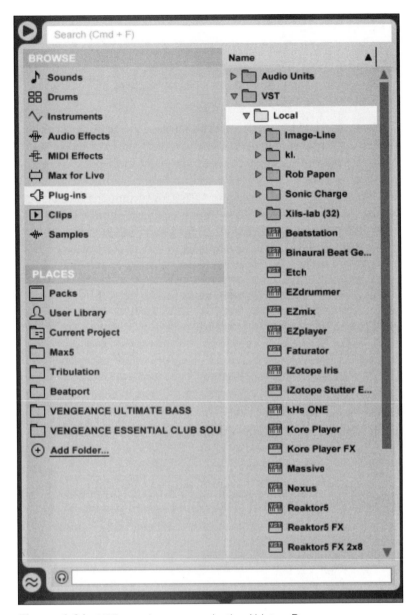

Figure 1.24 VSTs as they appear in the Ableton Browser.
Source: Ableton AG

> **32- AND 64-BIT PLUG-INS:** If a plug-in is missing, you may also double-check to ensure that you've downloaded the plug-in that is appropriate to the mode in which you're running. For example, if you're running in the 64-bit version of Live and you have a 32-bit plug-in installed, it won't appear. In Live's case, if you installed the 64-bit version of Live and you're running a 32-bit plug-in, it won't work. You may need to reinstall the 64-bit version of the plug-in if it's available, or install the 32-bit version of Live.

In the next chapter, we'll begin to get more familiar with the Browser, which is very, very handy. Now, let's talk about how to set up a Live template.

Setting Up Your Template

Granted, we're still early in our exploration of Live. But once you've gotten yourself more familiar with Live's functionality, you can return to this chapter and visit this section, which refers to setting up a Live template that suits your workflow.

1. Go to the very top of the File/Folder panel of Live's Preferences. You'll notice that the very first option/section is Save Current Set as Default, as shown in Figure 1.25.

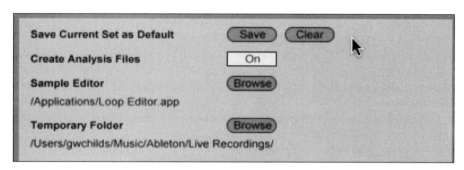

Figure 1.25 The Save Current Set as Default section as it appears in the File/Folder panel of Live Preferences. *Source:* Ableton AG

You'll notice two buttons in this small but significant section: the Save and Clear buttons. Let's talk about Save first. When you click the Save button, Live immediately assumes that the current Set in which you are working should now be the state that appears every time you open Live. So, needless to say, it's important that you click this button at a time when you are confident that the current state of your current Set is what you want to see each and every time you open Live.

If you clicked the Save button and have decided that you aren't happy with the Live template that appears by default, it's okay. You can easily mend this either by clicking the Save button again, when you have your Set in a state that would be desirable for a starting point every time you begin a new Set, or by clicking the Clear button. The Clear button will return the original template that was loaded the first time you started Ableton Live on your computer.

Again, I recommend you spend some time getting familiar with different instruments, effects, and so on before setting up a default template for Ableton Live. But if you already have an idea of what works for you, go ahead and experiment. It's not like you can't come back later and change it, right?

Setting Up Packs

Live has a really interesting way of adding expansions that include sounds, loops (in the form of clips) and instruments, and effects if you have Max for Live, which we'll get into in Chapter 8, "Specific Needs."

These expansions are known as *Packs*, and you can purchase them (or sometimes get them for free) from Ableton.com. If you're unsure of whether you have any available Packs for your version of Live, make sure you log in to your Ableton.com account and check out the Your Packs section of your Ableton account information. On this page, you can download and authorize existing Packs within your arsenal.

On the Your Packs page, shown in Figure 1.26, you'll notice that Packs that aren't currently on your computer will have a Download button next to them. This is an indication that you need to download the Pack. Once it's downloaded, the next time you go to the Your Packs page, there will be an Authorize button. You'll need to authorize the Pack before you can actually use the patches, clips, and instrument presets within it.

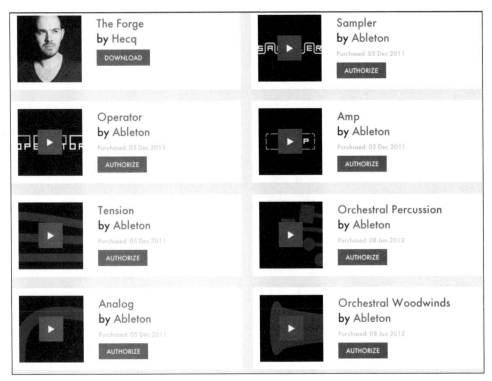

Figure 1.26 The Your Packs page of Ableton.com.
Source: Ableton AG

Let's go through the steps for installing a Pack now.

1. There is actually another way to do this. But for the moment, let's just stick to the most obvious method. We can talk about the other way later. Under the File menu in Ableton, select Install Pack, as shown in Figure 1.27.

Figure 1.27 The Install Pack function under the File menu.
Source: Ableton AG

2. Now locate the Live Pack that you downloaded (see Figure 1.28). If you just downloaded it and it's in your Downloads directory, that's fine, too. You don't need to move it; just locate and select it.

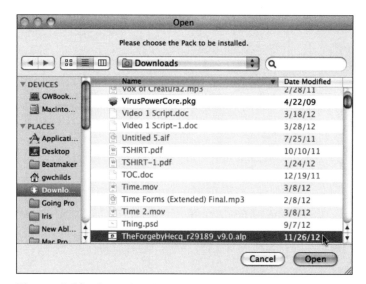

Figure 1.28 Browsing for a recently downloaded Live Pack.
Source: Ableton AG

3. Once you've selected the Pack, Live will begin installing it. The amount of time it takes will vary depending on how large the Pack is. When the download is complete, in most cases, you'll get some info on the Pack, if any was included. In my case, the Forge Pack has all the information on the sound designer, in the Help View of Ableton on the left. And the Pack is highlighted and opened within the Browser on the left. With the contents of the Pack revealed, I can see that I have instruments, clips, and specialized devices just for this Pack. See Figure 1.29.

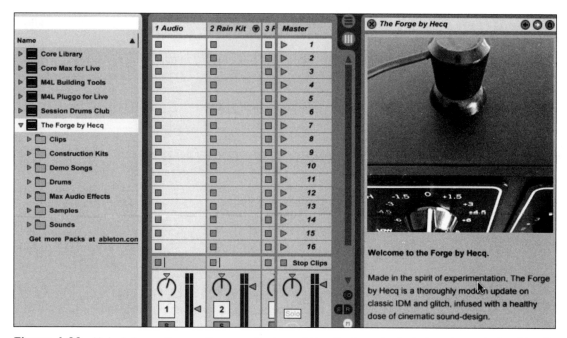

Figure 1.29 Help information on the new Pack, and the Pack contents being shown in the Live Browser.
Source: Ableton AG

4. Any Packs that you install will always have their location noted under the Packs location in Places, which appears inside the Live Browser, as shown in Figure 1.30. Whenever you're lacking sound inspiration, you need some clips that are just a little different, or you just want to experiment, click here.

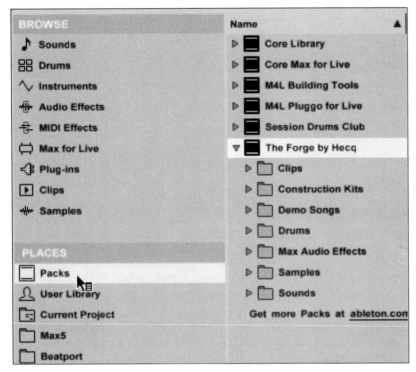

Figure 1.30 The Packs section of the Live Browser.

Source: Ableton AG

Packs ensure that the Live experience continues to grow as you move forward. Because they provide new sounds, instruments, MIDI effects, and more, you never know when the next Pack might change your entire workflow. And, if you're on the sound design/inventor side of the music spectrum, you'll be pleased to know that you can create your own Packs as well. See Chapter 8 for more information.

The Live Browser

We're not completely finished with setup, but it's a great time to continue our setup while incorporating an extremely important section of Ableton Live—the Browser. Not only does this section of Ableton give you access to all of your Ableton instruments, audio effects, and MIDI effects, but it also gives you access to your third-party plug-ins, samples, clips, and more.

Within the Live Browser, I'd like to start with Places. I draw your attention to this section first because I feel it's a place that even someone who is new to Live but has ample audio experience will put to use right away. And, it makes your existing sample libraries, effects libraries, drum libraries, and so on readily available.

Additionally, DJs who aspire to use Ableton Live will love Places because they can have all the directories where they store MP3s and such readily available to drag into Ableton.

Let's investigate a couple of ways to get your favorite music directories into Live now.

1. In the Places section of the Live Browser, click the Add Folder button. This tells Ableton Live that you have a new directory in mind for it. See Figure 1.31.

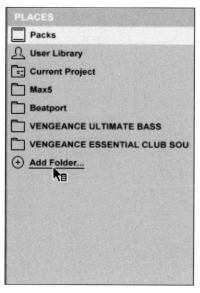

Figure 1.31 The Add Folder button within the Places section of the Live Browser.
Source: Ableton AG

2. A browser window will appear as soon as you click this button. Navigate to a folder that you'd like to have easy access to within Ableton Live's Places (see Figure 1.32). Again, think of sound presets for plug-ins, sample libraries, loop libraries, and directories filled with MP3s. The more you organize this area, the more fun you'll have. Trust me! When you have the folder that you want, click the Open button.

Figure 1.32 Guide Ableton to a directory that has samples, MP3s, and so on that you'll be using with Live.
Source: Ableton AG

3. Now that you've selected a folder, you'll notice that it appears within the Places section, as shown in Figure 1.33. And, if you click on this folder, you'll have access to the folder's contents within the Ableton Browser. You can now drag in MP3s, sampled loops, and samples to instruments like Simpler (see Chapter 3, "Arrangement and Session View").

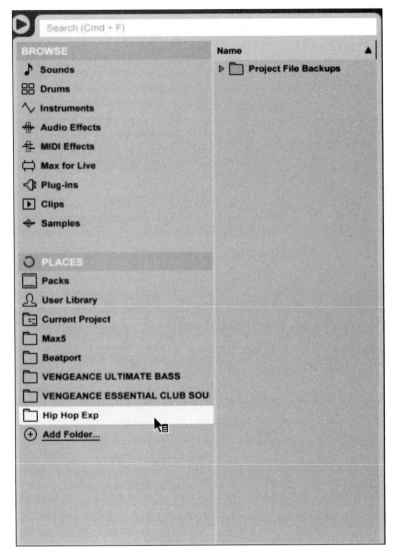

Figure 1.33 A custom folder as it appears in the Live Browser.
Source: Ableton AG

4. You probably also want to add some other folders. This time, let's do it a little differently. Open either an Explorer window (if you're on a PC) or Finder window (if you're on a Mac). Navigate to a folder or directory of folders that you'd like to have within Ableton Live's Browser.

5. Now that you've located one of your favorite directories, drag it from the Explorer or Finder window directly into Places. This has the same effect as using the Add Folder button. Also, feel free to drag a major directory, such as your Music folder, if it contains multiple subdirectories that you use. Or, drag the main directory and the subdirectories. The only warning I'll give is that you may not want to add too many options, or you might find yourself digging around more than you'd like. Keep it simple. See Figure 1.34.

Figure 1.34 Dragging a folder from a Finder window into the Places section of the Live Browser.
Source: Ableton AG

6. Now that you've got some of your own custom folders in the Places section of Ableton Live, let's try locating some audio and dragging it into the Arrangement View. To get to this view, press the Tab button. The Arrangement View, shown in Figure 1.35, as you'll soon discover in the next chapter, is very similar to the view in other DAWs, such as Pro Tools, Logic Pro, Cubase, Reaper, and so on. This is an area of Ableton Live where you can arrange, work with automation, and command the overall sequence of your entire performance. You'll notice within this view that there is actually an indicator telling you to Drag Files and Devices Here. Try this now—drag an audio file or MP3 where it says Drag Files and Devices Here.

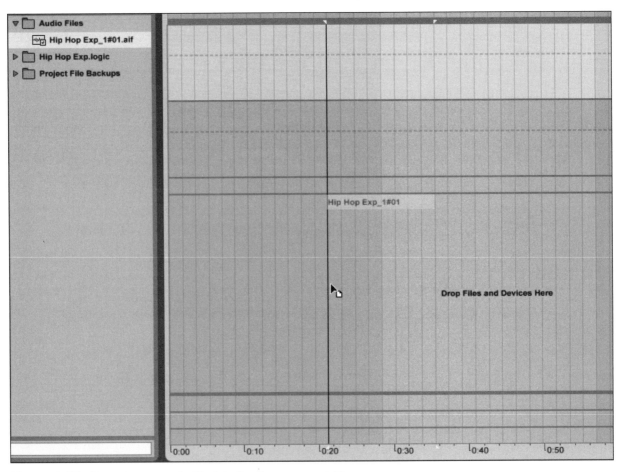

Figure 1.35 Dragging an audio file into the Arrangement View.
Source: Ableton AG

7. If all went well, you have an audio file sitting in your Arrangement View, like what you see in Figure 1.36. Try pressing the spacebar to play the audio file. You may need to single-click on the audio file so that Live knows where to begin. Either way, you're beginning to see how powerful it is to be able to so easily incorporate your own audio into this incredible platform for music production. Oh, and after you brought in the audio, you probably noticed Ableton doing a light amount of processing. This processing was Ableton trying to determine the audio's tempo and then warping the audio to suit the current host tempo. No other DAW works like it.

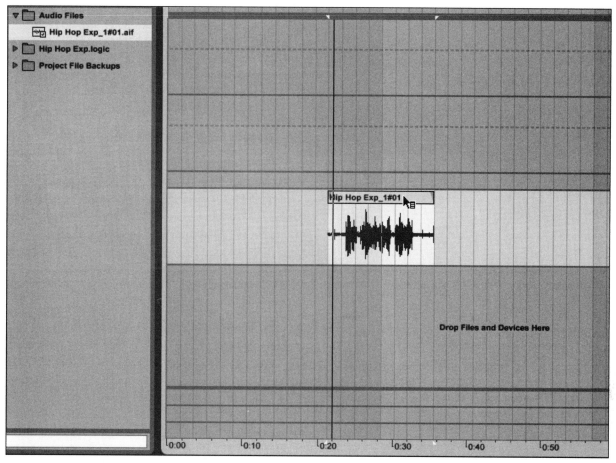

Figure 1.36 An audio file within the Arrangement View.
Source: Ableton AG

Conclusion

Okay, so you've got Ableton set up for the most part. You may still have some tweaks and things that you'd like to do, such as setting up a template and so on. Again, I still recommend getting to know Ableton a little more before you do this. There are a lot of powerful tools that may not have existed in the DAWs you've used in the past.

In the next chapter, we're going to go deeper into the Browser and the Arrangement View. With this next chapter, you'll be armed with the tools you need to start basic recording with Ableton, as well as some choice instruments that will get you started.

Ableton Production Basics

2

I N THE PREVIOUS CHAPTER, you learned about the important background features that help you keep your Ableton experience stable and fun. You also took an important step toward music creation, the Ableton Browser, which really is the nexus of all tools for working with Live.

In this chapter, you'll delve further into the Browser and learn how it allows you to easily and quickly get the effects, instruments, and loops you need to begin creating and, most importantly, recording your music.

In addition to learning more about the Browser, you'll also focus on recording and using Live's mixer and its assorted functions in relation to pro audio recording.

You'll be excited to know that Live's method of recording audio isn't limited to recording mere loops. You can record full audio tracks the same way that you can in Pro Tools, Cubase, Logic Pro, and so on. Live is a full-featured DAW. However, the Session View, which is only *one* view in Ableton, often leads people to believe that it's something of a toy. Do not be misled! Because the Session View can easily throw people off, let's focus on the view that is most similar to other DAWs—the Arrangement View.

In the previous chapter, where you first visited the Arrangement View, you dragged an audio file into the view. By the time you finish this chapter, you'll be recording in the Arrangement View.

Let's start now with exploring basic audio effects and how to assign them to an audio track.

Browser/Effect Exercise

Any recording engineer will want easy access to corrective and creative effects. In this exercise, you'll learn how accessible the Live effects and your plug-in effects are. Seriously, ask and you shall receive.

Let's start this simple exercise now; you'll learn how to ask for, find, and remove effects in Ableton. For this simple exercise, you'll be working in the Arrangement View, so make sure you press Tab and work in the view that you began utilizing in the previous chapter.

1. Click on Audio Effects in the Browser (see Figure 2.1). This will quickly display all of the Ableton Live internal effects devices. If you look down the list that appears next to the Browse box, you'll notice several mainstay audio effects like Compressors, Gates, Filters, and so on.

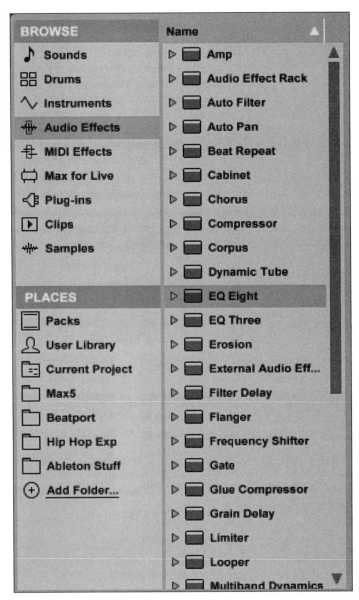

Figure 2.1 Audio effects as they appear in the Ableton Browser.
Source: Ableton AG

2. As you can see, it's extremely easy to find what you're looking for. But, let's take this a step further. Try the keyboard shortcut Command+F (Ctrl+F if you're on a PC). When you use this shortcut, you put the Browser into a search mode. Now try typing **Compressor** (see Figure 2.2). Instantly, a Compressor will appear. What's nice about this shortcut is that it's quicker than having to move your cursor over and start looking around for effects. Simply press Command/Ctrl+F and type in what you need.

Figure 2.2 The Ableton Browser in Search mode.
Source: Ableton AG

3. Now that you see how to access effects, let's assign the effect as an insert to an audio track. Use the shortcut Command/Ctrl+T to create a new audio track (see Figure 2.3). Audio tracks allow you to record vocals, guitar, and so on—essentially, anything that incorporates a microphone or a "real" instrument. We'll get to MIDI tracks later. By default, an audio track or a MIDI track will already be created, but this is good so you get the feel for using the very handy shortcut.

Figure 2.3 Creating an audio track in Ableton's Arrangement View.
Source: Ableton AG

4. Now, with the Compressor still in the Browser search, double-click the actual device known as Compressor. Your new audio track will automatically be selected because it was just created, and the Compressor will be assigned instantly to this track. You'll know this to be true because you'll see the Compressor device at the bottom of the screen, as shown in Figure 2.4.

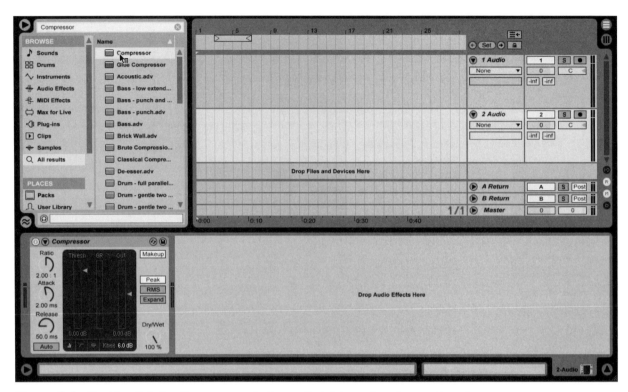

Figure 2.4 Double-click the Compressor device so that it is assigned as an insert.
Source: Ableton AG

5. Now let's take one step back, just to prove a point. Because Ableton's effects and instruments are added differently from those in most DAWs, let's learn another way to add and remove plug-ins. First, remove the Compressor that you just created. You'll currently see the Compressor in the lower-left corner of Live, near the Help box, if you have it enabled. Click the title bar, where it says Compressor, as shown in Figure 2.5, and press Delete on your QWERTY keyboard. This will remove the Compressor from the track as an insert.

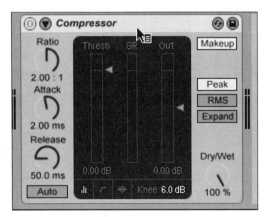

Figure 2.5 Click the title bar of the Compressor effect to remove it.
Source: Ableton AG

6. Now let's re-add the Compressor to the same track, but I'll show you a different way to do it. With the Compressor still listed in the Ableton Browser, drag the Compressor from the Browser on to the audio track you created in previous steps. You can drop the effect either on the title bar of the created audio track or in the area where the Compressor was sitting earlier, before you deleted it (see Figure 2.6). Because the editor area below changes based on your current focus, I usually drag to the track's title bar when I use the drag-and-drop method.

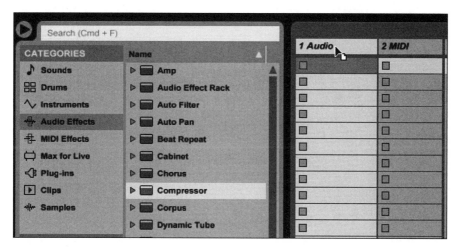

Figure 2.6 Drag an effect to an audio track in Ableton.
Source: Ableton AG

In this very simple exercise, you learned some basics that you will use throughout Ableton Live. From this exercise, you learned to quickly find, apply, and remove effects. And the good news is, all plug-ins, instruments, and effects are removed and applied in the same way in Ableton. So, going forward, when I ask you to add an instrument, you'll already know exactly how to do it!

All right, now it's time to start looking at how to record audio in the Arrangement View. Save your progress if you haven't already, and then continue to the next exercise.

Arrangement View: Recording the First Audio Track

In this exercise, we'll conquer the most important task for any DAW: recording audio. We'll begin doing this in the Arrangement View, because it's likely the most similar to recording in other DAWs you've worked with in the past. You may find yourself using this method a lot as you get familiar with using Ableton. But I urge you to continue forward from this exercise after you finish it. Once you start using Session View recording techniques, you might find the Arrangement View method a little antiquated.

For this exercise, you'll record multiple tracks of audio, so make sure you save periodically. You'll also want to have a microphone connected to your audio interface for this exercise—and instruments, if you prefer. I will be using the microphone to "beat-box" drums and hum a bass part. Is Ableton intended only for recorded audio? Of course not! In fact, some of the audio that we record won't even be audio when we're finished.

Going Pro with Ableton Live

1. Before you can do any recording, you need to select the input that the microphone is coming into on your audio interface. To do so, you'll need to access the I-O section available on every track in Ableton—although MIDI will appear differently from audio, for obvious reasons. To access the input section of your audio track, make sure the I-O button, shown in Figure 2.7, is highlighted. In fact, you may want to toggle it on and off a few times to see what appears and disappears in the tracks when you do this.

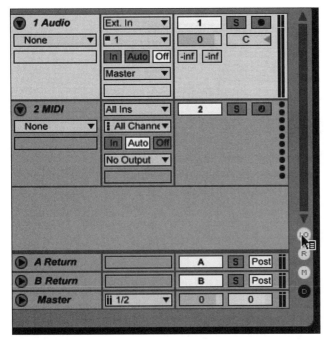

Figure 2.7 Enable the I-O section in Ableton's Arrangement View.
Source: Ableton AG

2. In the I-O, or In/Out, section of each audio track, you have access to the inputs and outputs for each audio track, as shown in Figure 2.8. So, you can choose what audio input you'll be using to record for each track, and you can also choose whether this track will go to the Master track of Ableton or to an external output. The very top drop-down menu of the I-O section selects the source device. For example, suppose you have two audio interfaces. The second drop-down box allows you to select the specific input on the device you chose in the top drop-down menu. The bottom drop-down box has you determine your output. For the moment, select the device and input using the first and second drop-down menus in the I-O section of the audio track in which you'll be recording.

Figure 2.8 The I-O section of the Ableton audio track.
Source: Ableton AG

3. If the input you selected is working properly and there is a mic or an instrument attached, you'll notice that the levels will be moving in the small drop-down menu from which you selected your input. However, you may notice you aren't hearing any sound. First, the Monitoring section, shown in Figure 2.9, may be set to Off or Auto. When Auto is on, input monitoring takes place only when the track is armed. In should be applied when you want monitoring for this track to be active all the time, regardless of whether it's armed. For the moment, select Auto as your monitoring preference and ensure that the track is armed, also shown in Figure 2.9.

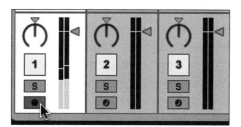

Figure 2.9 The monitoring section of an Ableton audio track, and the track being armed.
Source: Ableton AG

HEADPHONES: If you're on a laptop, you may notice severe feedback when monitoring is enabled. If this is the case, I highly recommend connecting a pair of headphones; speakers in the laptop will exacerbate the situation because they are so close to the built-in mic.

---

4. Now, with your audio track set up to record, there's only one thing missing: a metronome. In the upper-left corner of Ableton's interface, you'll notice an odd button with a white and a black dot in it. Press this button to enable the click track when recording time comes. If you click on the small drop-down menu directly to the right of the button, you can select whether you want a 1- to 4-bar count-in. See Figure 2.10.

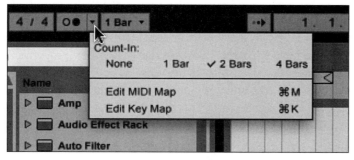

Figure 2.10 The Metronome button and its pre-count options.
Source: Ableton AG

5. All right, it's finally time to record! Press the F9 button to begin recording. This button on your QWERTY keyboard triggers the Arrangement Record button, which rests at the top of Ableton's interface, near the Play and Stop buttons, shown in Figure 2.11. For this audio track, I suggest recording yourself beat-boxing a drum beat. If your beat-boxing skills are rusty, as mine are, make sure you are in a private environment where you won't be embarrassed. If you can't—or won't—beat-box, record yourself tapping on a desk in rhythm. The point is to take a rough piece of percussion. Make sure you do something like this, because it's important for later exercises. When you are finished recording, simply press the spacebar on your QWERTY keyboard.

Figure 2.11 The Record button, within the transport bar, at the top of Ableton's Arrangement View.

Source: Ableton AG

6. At this point, you should be the proud owner of a recorded beat within Ableton Live. It may not be a polished beat—we'll get to that part later—but it's a percussive beat produced by either your mouth or your fingers. To play the part back, simply press the spacebar again. Or, to play starting from a specific point in the recording, click within the audio click where you would like the recording to start. Doing this will place a small, glowing line, known as the *arrangement insert marker*, shown in Figure 2.12. This marker is used for many purposes, but for the moment, let's just regard it as a way to cue a specific region within the Arrangement View. Try positioning this arrangement insert marker in a few positions within your recording and then stopping and starting with the spacebar.

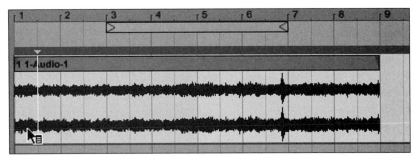

Figure 2.12 Ableton's arrangement insert marker.

Source: Ableton AG

7. When you've got a feel for working with the transport, let's take a look at a function that is very important for building your arrangements, grooves, and melodies. Like all DAWs, Ableton has a standard Loop mode where the sequencer cycles over and over a specific set of measures. This is very different from the looped clips and the way they work within the Session View, but we'll get to that later. Let's stick with what you know first. Before looping, check to see whether your recorded clip's length is even, so that it will loop properly. For example, if the recorded audio clip is nine measures long, trim it to eight measures so it will loop without a hitch. Trimming is really easy: Simply move your mouse cursor to the upper-left corner of the audio clip. Hover around this area until the cursor changes to a], as shown in Figure 2.13. Once this appears, drag the corner of the loop to the left. This will resize the clip to fit within a standard timeline.

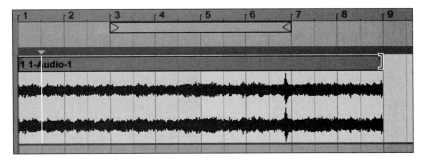

Figure 2.13 Resizing an audio clip in Ableton's Arrangement View.

Source: Ableton AG

8. Now that the clip is sized to an even number, let me show you how to set up Loop mode in the Arrangement View. Click on the audio clip's colored bar, so that the whole clip is highlighted, as shown in Figure 2.14. When the whole clip appears highlighted, use the shortcut Command+L (Ctrl+L on the PC). Now the Ableton sequencer will loop only within this area of the arrangement. You'll also see loop brackets, similar to the way that they appear in most sequencers, framing your audio clip.

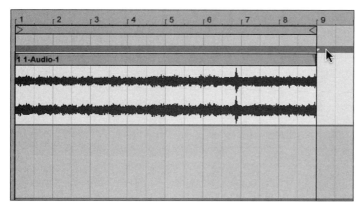

Figure 2.14 Looping an audio clip in Ableton's Arrangement View.
Source: Ableton AG

9. Okay, you've got a nice, rough, percussive beat looping and cut. Now let's make it sound good by converting it into something a little more usable. Ableton has a few really remarkable audio-to-MIDI conversion functions that can make production and creation a fun experience. Keep in mind, these functions will not capture and re-create the audio exactly. But with careful editing and an open mind, you can get some choice drum beats. Try this now: Right-click on your beat-boxed audio clip and select Convert Drums to New MIDI Track, as shown in Figure 2.15.

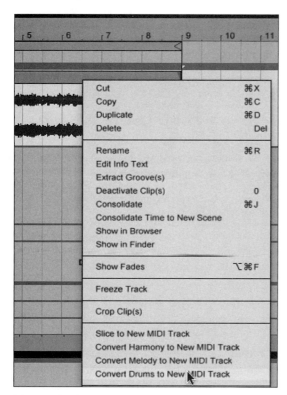

Figure 2.15 Selecting Convert Drums to New MIDI Track from the contextual menu.
Source: Ableton AG

Once this option is selected, you'll notice that a progress bar will appear in the middle of the screen, as shown in Figure 2.16. Depending on the length of the clip you're converting, this bar can be longer or shorter in the amount of time it takes to complete. But what happens when completion occurs is very, very cool. Now that processing is finished, a second track will appear with not an audio clip, but a MIDI clip. Assigned to this MIDI clip, as an instrument, is a Drum Rack—an Ableton proprietary instrument that is actually made up of several sample playback devices in a cluster. Each sample playback device is filled with a drum sample. The main thing to know about the Drum Rack at this point is that it is a full drum kit assigned to your track. You don't have to worry about it. If you don't like the drum sounds, don't worry—we'll change those out later. It's MIDI; you aren't locked in to specific instruments. That's the beauty of it! See Figure 2.17, in which you'll see my Drum Rack and MIDI clip, created from the audio clip in the previous steps.

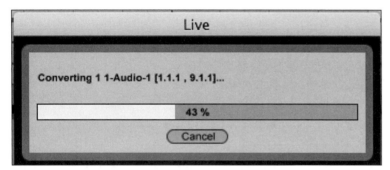

Figure 2.16 The progress bar for the Convert Drums to New MIDI Track function.
Source: Ableton AG

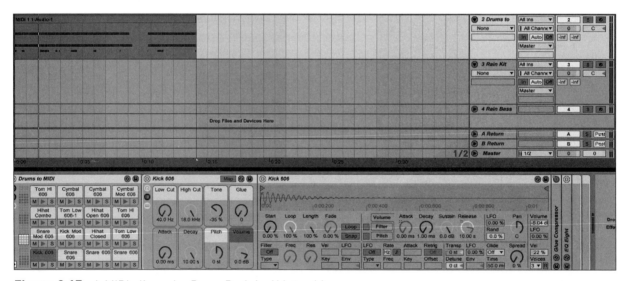

Figure 2.17 A MIDI clip and a Drum Rack in Ableton Live.
Source: Ableton AG

10. Of course, you're probably eager to hear how a computer has reinterpreted your beat-boxing or desk-drumming. That is the whole point of this step. You can mute the original audio track, which houses the clip you had Ableton convert, by disabling the Track Activator button. These buttons are the numbered buttons that appear on every track. You simply press the number button for the track, and it toggles on or off. Alternatively, you can solo the MIDI clip that was created from your audio clip by pressing the S button on your audio track. Figure 2.18 shows both buttons. However, if neither button currently appears on your end,

make sure you toggle the Show/Hide Mixer button, shown in Figure 2.19. Go ahead and play the MIDI clip on its own and start getting an idea of what you'd like to fix.

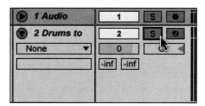

Figure 2.18 The Mixer section as it appears in the Ableton Arrangement View.
Source: Ableton AG

Figure 2.19 The Show/Hide Mixer toggle.
Source: Ableton AG

11. So, what do you think? Is Ableton sad or spectacular? Did it reinterpret your beat-boxing/drumming in a way that does it justice, or does it need work? In most cases, you'll want to do light or even serious editing. And I'll tell you that for future reference, as you use the Convert Drums to New MIDI Track function, you'll want to get as clean of a recording as possible. But for the moment, it's giving us great editing fodder! Let's take a look at the MIDI editor now. To access the MIDI editor, double-click on the MIDI clip in the Arrangement View. The MIDI editor will appear at the bottom of the screen where the Drum Rack panel used to appear. See Figure 2.20.

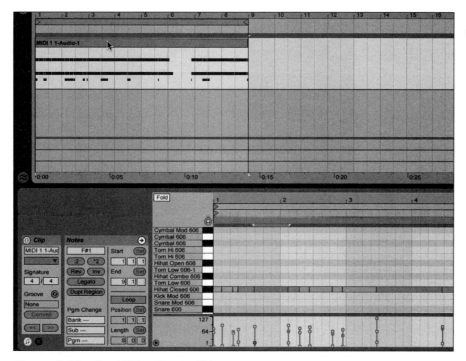

Figure 2.20 The MIDI editor in Ableton.
Source: Ableton AG

12. You may notice that the MIDI editor isn't showing enough of the note data that you require for editing. To increase the size of the editor, you can hover your mouse over the dividing line between the Arrangement View and the editor. The cursor will change to two arrows pointing up and down, as shown in Figure 2.21. Click on the line when this cursor icon appears and drag up. The editor size will increase. You can also hover your cursor inside the editor, where all the notes are, and scroll up and down with your mouse wheel or similar function. The editor will, in turn, scroll up and down.

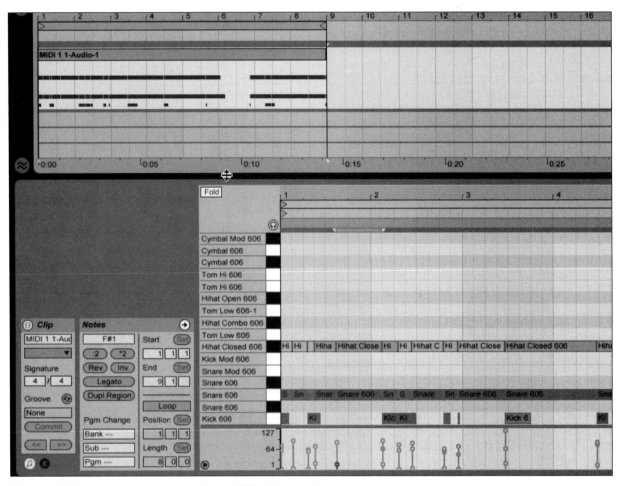

Figure 2.21 Expanding the size of the MIDI editor window.
Source: Ableton AG

13. Now that you have full access to the MIDI data of your new MIDI drum part, you'll undoubtedly have a few edits in mind. Editing MIDI in Live couldn't be easier! Before you begin, however, let's make Ableton do one more minor job for you. Quantize! Click once inside the MIDI editor window and do a Select All, or press Command/Ctrl+A (see Figure 2.22). This will select every note within your clip.

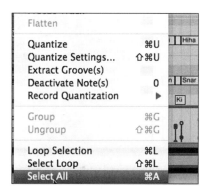

Figure 2.22 Selecting all the notes within the MIDI editor.
Source: Ableton AG

14. Now, with everything selected, go up to the Edit menu in Ableton Live and choose Quantize Settings. Within the dialog box that appears, select 1/16 from the drop-down menu and keep the Amount value at 100% (see Figure 2.23). Or, if you're not a fan of really intense quantization, adjust to a setting that works for you. Click the OK button at the bottom, and Ableton will do its quantization function. Note that once you've done this in the Quantize Settings, you can use the Command/Ctrl+U shortcut to quantize at the selected settings any time you want.

Figure 2.23 Quantizing in Ableton Live.
Source: Ableton AG

15. Now that you're quantized, it's time to get rid of any erroneous MIDI data that isn't working for you. Simply double-click on a note to delete any note you do not want (see Figure 2.24). At the same time, if you double-click in an empty area, you will create new notes. You can also drag to select multiple notes and press Delete to get rid of clumps of MIDI data you don't want. Try removing notes you do not want within your MIDI drum clip. Don't worry about adding anything yet. We'll get to that in the next step.

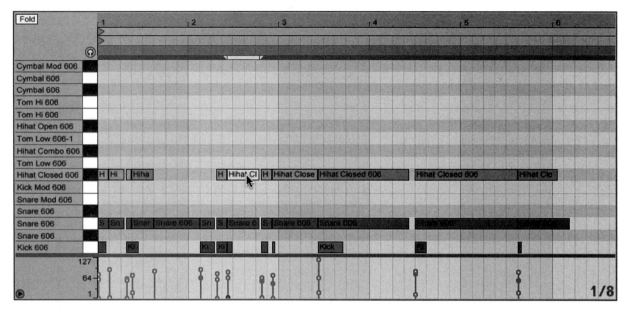

Figure 2.24 Removing notes in Ableton's MIDI editor.

Source: Ableton AG

16. After removing what you don't want within your drum clip, you've probably started to get ideas for what you *do* want. An easy way to add multiple notes, such as a 16-beat hi-hat rhythm, is to use the Pencil tool, also known as Draw mode (see Figure 2.25). Press the B button on your QWERTY keyboard to slip into and out of this mode. With the Draw mode in action, you can click and drag to draw in multiple notes. The length that is drawn depends on your grid settings. Command/Ctrl+1, 2, or 3 will cause the grid to get bigger or smaller. Experiment with drawing in multiple notes with different grid sizes. I promise, you'll get some nice drum patterns when you experiment with the different grid sizes.

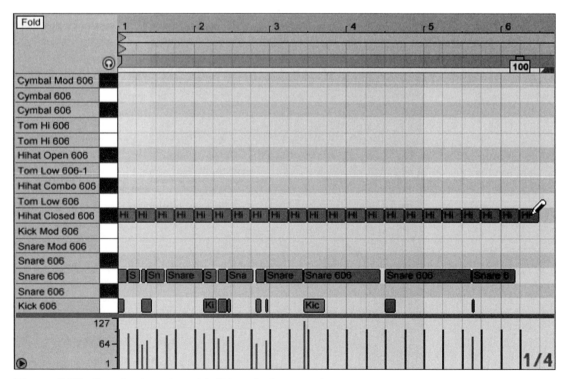

Figure 2.25 Drawing in notes with Ableton's Draw mode.

Source: Ableton AG

17. While drawing in notes, you may want to be able to hear what you're drawing in. Ableton has a preview function within every editor in the program—even in the Browser—which we'll get to later. Click the Preview button to enable this feature (see Figure 2.26). Trust me, it makes the job much easier than having to press Play over and over again, or continually looping without knowing what you're entering.

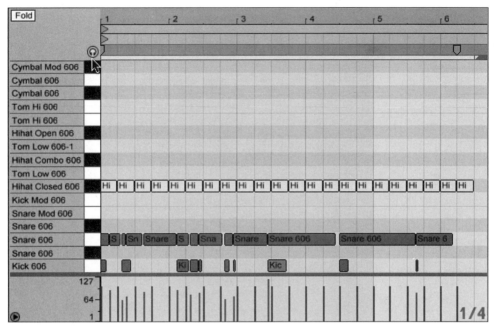

Figure 2.26 Enabling preview in Ableton's MIDI editor.
Source: Ableton AG

18. When you have your drum clip sounding the way you like within the loop points you set up earlier, let's move to making a new audio track that can act as a bass part for what you've created so far. Again, use your microphone to create this part. Either you can hum in the part that you'd like to add to the drum beat or you can use an instrument, such as a bass guitar. Use Command/Ctrl+T to make a new audio track, set up your input, and record the way you did earlier in this chapter. You may want to disable Loop mode while recording in the new part. To do this, click the Loop button at the top of Ableton's interface, as shown in Figure 2.27. Once you've completed your hummed bass recording, move to the next step.

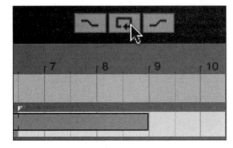

Figure 2.27 Disabling Loop mode.
Source: Ableton AG

19. Now that you have a hummed bass part, let's convert it to MIDI as well. The method for doing this is very similar to Convert Drums to New MIDI Track—the function we used earlier for our drum loop. However, for the bass part, we'll use Convert Melody to New MIDI Track. This function is reserved for audio that plays

only individual notes at a time. For example, a bass guitar will usually play one note at a time, as opposed to chords that overlap one another. Right-click on your new recorded audio part and select Convert Melody to New MIDI Track, as shown in Figure 2.28.

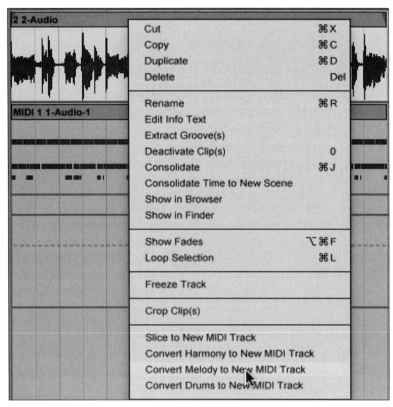

Figure 2.28 Converting audio with the Convert Melody to New MIDI Track function.
Source: Ableton AG

20. All right, because you're starting to add on some tracks, it might be a good time to organize what you have. First, give the tracks names that are more indicative of their content. Label the track with the recorded percussion, or beat-boxing, that you created at the beginning of this chapter *Drum Audio*. You can do this by clicking on the track title and using the shortcut Command/Ctrl+R. Then, type in the name you'd prefer. Label the audio track you used to create a MIDI bass *Bass Audio*. Label the MIDI drums *MIDI Drums*, and the MIDI bass *MIDI Bass*. See Figure 2.29.

Figure 2.29 Labeling the audio and MIDI tracks.
Source: Ableton AG

21. Because you're not really using the audio tracks, after converting them you may want to just group them and stow them for later. Grouping tracks in Ableton is useful for several purposes. For example, you can group all of your vocal tracks to create a submix. For the moment, let's just use this as a way to tidy up. Hold down the Shift button and select both audio tracks. Then, use the Command/Ctrl+G function to group the audio tracks. After grouping, label the Group track *Source Audio*, as shown in Figure 2.30. You can also press the small arrow next to the Group track name to condense the Group track, thus creating room.

Figure 2.30 Group track in Ableton.
Source: Ableton AG

22. Now re-enable the Loop function and mute the grouped audio track, so that you can hear how well Ableton reinterpreted your bass part. Most likely, it will need editing, and you know how to do that now. But after editing, you may decide that you really want only a portion of the MIDI that was made available from the audio. For example, perhaps there's one riff that you'd like to repeat. Try this out: Edit the MIDI Bass track to the point that you like it, using the steps we went through earlier. Then, drag to select the portion of the clip that you don't want, as shown in Figure 2.31, and press Delete. This will immediately trim the clip in a way that is very similar to other DAWs you've probably worked with.

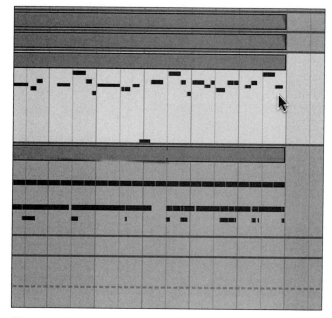

Figure 2.31 Drag-selecting a portion of a clip.
Source: Ableton AG

23. Because the clip is nicely trimmed now, you should repeat the part, as it's a bass part. We need a little repetition. Click on your newly edited bass clip, hold down the Option (Mac) or Alt button (PC), and drag the clip over. When you let go of the clip, you'll notice that a new copy has been created, as shown in Figure 2.32.

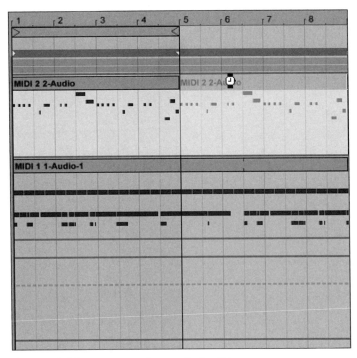

Figure 2.32 Drag-copying a clip in Ableton.
Source: Ableton AG

24. With the bass dialed in, in terms of what it's playing, it might be nice to get a bass patch for the actual MIDI part. The one that we have currently is okay, but come on—we can do better than this, right? Here's another chance to take a look at a very good Browser function known as *Hot Swap*. This function works for more than just instruments. As a matter of fact, it works with effects, instruments, and even grooves, which we'll get into later. For the moment, though, you can get it to help you find a batter bass patch. Press the Q button to enter Hot Swap mode while the bass MIDI track is selected, as shown in Figure 2.33. Once you're in Hot Swap mode, start playing your looped region within the Ableton Arrangement View. You might as well hear the patch with the part that's being played.

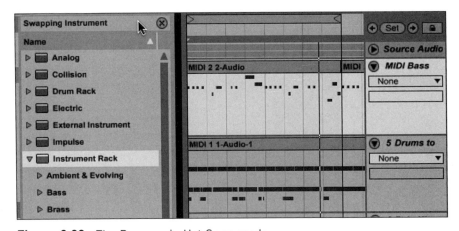

Figure 2.33 The Browser in Hot Swap mode.
Source: Ableton AG

25. Now that you have the looped region playing, try out some different bass patches. Use the Command/Ctrl+F shortcut to search while in Hot Swap mode, and type in **Bass**, as shown in Figure 2.34. This will allow you to narrow your search to basses only.

Figure 2.34 Searching with the Browser.
Source: Ableton AG

26. As you type, you'll notice that Ableton begins to look for patches that match the description. The category currently selected will also greatly affect which bass patches you will see. For example, if you choose the Instruments category in the Browser, folders will appear for Ableton instruments only. But if you open those folders, you will see bass patches only for these instruments, as shown in Figure 2.35. You can also choose the All Results category, which will, of course, show you everything bass—even effects intended for bass. I suggest trying out the different bass patches in the Instruments category. To audition different patches, simply double-click on the patch you'd like to try. This will load up the patch instantly. You may also want to keep your project looping, so that you can hear the patch changes as they occur. Find a patch that you like.

Figure 2.35 Choosing a bass patch.
Source: Ableton AG

27. At this point, you may have come to the conclusion that the drums you set up earlier don't exactly match the style you prefer. And the Browser is more than handy at helping you find replacement kits that sound great. However, when it comes to drums, the Find function that we used to find the bass can be a little misleading. For example, if you tried to do a search for just "drums," you'd be greeted by loads of samples, loops, and so

on. But if you look within the Categories section, you'll notice that there is, in fact, a Drums category, and it shows you all of the Ableton kits available.

Just select Drums and move down the list. Try using the Hot Swap command to try out different drum kits. Select the MIDI Drums track we set up earlier, and then press the Q button. Because a Drum Rack is already in place, the Hot Swap function will cause the Browser to jump to the Drums category automatically. But what's even cooler is that you're about to discover that you can even preview kits without having to assign the drum patch to the MIDI track.

You'll notice that in the lowest section of the Browser, there is a small panel that has a Preview button next to it, as shown in Figure 2.36. If the Preview button is enabled in the Browser, you can simply select a kit, synth patch, loop, and so on. Once it's selected, you'll hear an audio representation of the patch. This is extremely handy, especially if you're a DJ. I'll explain more as we get further into the book. For now, try selecting different kits with the Hot Swap function (Q) and previewing kits in the Browser.

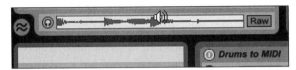

Figure 2.36 Previewing in the Ableton Browser.
Source: Ableton AG

Conclusion

We've covered a lot in this chapter. In fact, aside from automation, which we'll get into in Chapter 5, "Mix and Effects," we've covered a great deal of what the Arrangement View is all about. I think you'll agree that it's not really that different from what you've already worked with. And, you'll be happy to know that it does incorporate many of the must-have features that other DAWs incorporate, such as markers (known as *Locators* in Ableton Live). As we move forward, we'll get into those in the next chapter. And the next chapter will begin our foray into the exotic Session View.

See you in the next chapter!

3

Arrangement and Session View

Now that you're familiar with the Arrangement View in Ableton Live, you're probably already connecting the dots about how you're going to use it. But I encourage you to spend some time in this chapter before you come up with any concrete plans.

In this chapter, we'll continue with the Arrangement View, but we'll also move forward to unknown territory and the features that really set Ableton apart from any other DAW. In fact, these are the features that may have made you hesitant to approach Ableton in the first place. But I can assure you that after spending time with the previous chapter and this one, you'll start to see why so many people—both professionals and enthusiasts—have switched to this amazing product.

It's important to note that you'll be continuing from the work you did in the previous chapter. So load up your work if you need to, or just continue with what you already have.

In this chapter, you'll finish learning about the audio-to-MIDI conversion possibilities in Ableton and then move on to the Session View, as well as learn about how Live mixes, handles loops, and so much more.

All right, let's begin!

From Arrangement to Session

In the previous chapter, you spent a lot of time converting audio to MIDI and then editing. And even though it seemed like we covered a lot, we didn't cover everything. In fact, there's one more really fascinating audio-to-MIDI conversion technique, and it will be the building block for this particular tutorial.

You'll want to continue with what you built in the previous chapter, so if you don't have that available already, pull it up now.

This particular audio-to-MIDI conversion technique will require a different type of musical audio to work as it's supposed to. The ideal situation would be to record yourself playing a guitar or piano. If you have an instrument like a guitar or piano already, set up your inputs in Session View, as you did in the previous chapter, and begin recording.

If you don't have an instrument to record with, that's fine. You can use Ableton's virtual instruments to cheat the system. Granted, you'll be recording MIDI initially. But you can easily turn MIDI into audio, as you'll see.

1. To get the virtual instrument going, create a MIDI track using Command/Ctrl+Shift+T. After you do that, use the Command/Ctrl+F shortcut to do a search for pianos. When you find a piano you like, drag it onto the MIDI track that you created, as shown in Figure 3.1.

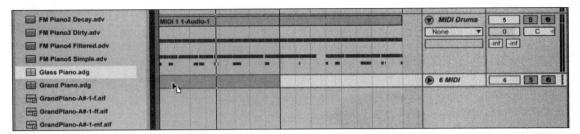

Figure 3.1 Create a MIDI track in Ableton's Arrangement View.
Source: Ableton AG

2. Now that you have a piano instrument assigned, you can start recording your MIDI data. Make sure that the track is armed, as shown in Figure 3.2, and then click the Record button to start recording your MIDI piano part.

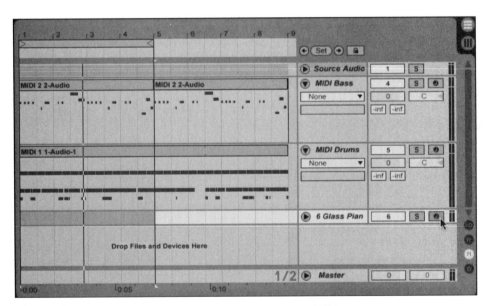

Figure 3.2 Press the Record button to record a new MIDI sequence.
Source: Ableton AG

NO MIDI CONTROLLER: If you don't have a MIDI controller when you're working through these tutorials, don't worry. Live has a really nice QWERTY functionality. Make sure that the keyboard button (also known as the *Computer MIDI Keyboard toggle*) in the upper-right corner is pressed, or lit up, as shown in Figure 3.3. With the Keyboard button on, simply press keys on the line of A–L to play the white keys; keys on the row of W–O are the black keys. Use the Z and X buttons to go up and down octaves. It's also important to note that the Computer MIDI Keyboard is polyphonic, which means you can play chords for this exercise. Make sure you play inside the looped/cycled region that you set up in the previous chapter. You may need to set up the loop points again using the Command/Ctrl+L function.

Figure 3.3 The Computer MIDI Keyboard toggle in Ableton Live.
Source: Ableton AG

3. Now that you've got a polyphonic, chorded part set up within the arrangement, you can convert it to audio—so that you can later convert it back to MIDI. This might seem confusing, but you're learning important functionality within Ableton Live. Create an audio track using the Command/Ctrl+T shortcut. Set the input of this track to be the MIDI track that has the piano on it. For example, if the MIDI track is labeled Glass Piano (which is the instrument I used), choose that as the input for your audio track. See Figure 3.4. You can select the input in the I-O section of the audio track. You can, of course, toggle this section off and on using the I-O section toggle button to the lower right, also shown in Figure 3.4.

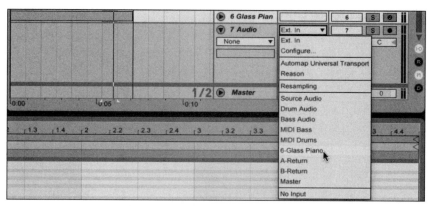

Figure 3.4 Setting up the inputs on an audio track within the track's I-O section.
Source: Ableton AG

4. When you're ready, cue the MIDI piano part so that it starts at the beginning and then arm the audio track that has the MIDI piano set up as the input. When you click the Record button, you'll have the MIDI track piping directly into the audio track. And yes, there are other ways of converting MIDI to audio. But with this method, you're getting to see a very interesting bit of functionality within Ableton—the bussing system. When you get near the end of the MIDI part, stop recording, as shown in Figure 3.5.

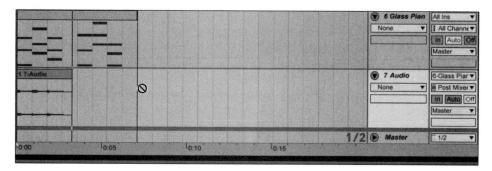

Figure 3.5 Recording MIDI as an audio track.
Source: Ableton AG

5. Because you have successfully converted MIDI to audio, let's take a look at the last of the audio-to-MIDI conversion functions—Convert Harmony to New MIDI Track. I hope that you actually had a guitar or an external instrument, such as a piano, or even a guitar loop, because it's the best way to experience this feature. If not, perhaps you'll get some mileage out of this feature in the future. Either way, right-click on the audio part you just created and select Convert Harmony to New MIDI Track. This function, unlike Convert Melody to New MIDI Track, actually analyzes and replicates chords and notes that stack on top of one another. Like the other Convert functions, it's not perfect. You will find yourself doing a little editing after even the most pristine recordings. But if you have the patience, this function can be amazing for MIDI-fying guitars and actually making them sound real later, as you apply virtual guitar patches. Trust me: In other applications, this isn't easy to do.

Once you've finished the audio-to-MIDI conversion, edit your part so that it sounds right to your ears, as shown in Figure 3.6.

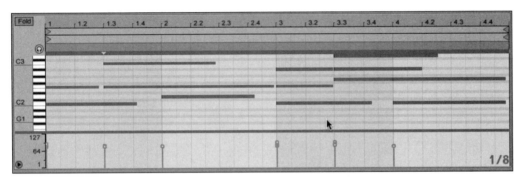

Figure 3.6 Editing MIDI after converting harmony to MIDI.
Source: Ableton AG

6. After you have your "harmony," as Ableton calls it, together, shift your attention to a new section of Ableton that you will spend a lot of time with once you get to know it. I think how we're going to transition to it will make you very happy. Before you go there, let me show you a function that will help you transition there very easily. First consider the duration of the clips that you've been building thus far. Try to choose from an even number, because these clips will be looping later. So, select a clip starting from Measure 1, all the way to Measures 8, 16, 32, and so on. See Figure 3.7.

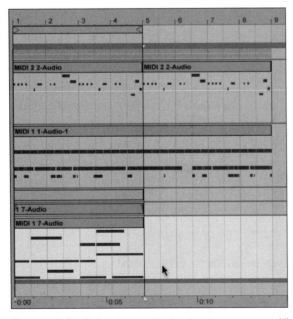

Figure 3.7 Selecting a clip in the Arrangement View.
Source: Ableton AG

7. Once you've selected the appropriate duration for the clips you've been working with so far, go to the Create menu and select Consolidate Time to New Scene, as shown in Figure 3.8. This is an extremely cool function that you'll use a lot, especially if you get into remixing, mashups, and more. It's a tool that takes clips in the Arrangement View and makes new copies of the appropriate length in the Session View. If you have audio in this selection, Ableton will re-export the audio, trimmed to the length that you've selected. When the Consolidate Time to New Scene function has finished, press the Tab button to see your handiwork.

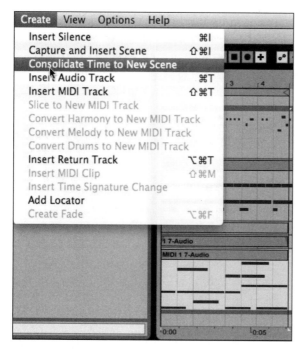

Figure 3.8 Select the Consolidate Time to New Scene feature from the Ableton Create menu.
Source: Ableton AG

Welcome to Session View. This view can take some getting used to if you're used to more linear sequencers, as found in Cubase, Logic Pro, Pro Tools, and so on. Don't let this intimidate you, as you'll be spending a lot of time here. And believe me, once you get used to it, you might wonder why you ever used the sequencers that I mentioned previously.

Session View is a lot of fun. First notice the clips that you've brought over from the Arrangement View. You'll notice that the tracks correspond perfectly to what you'll see in the Arrangement View, if you were to press the Tab button to toggle back there. The tracks are in the exact same order and have almost the exact same clips. Part of the reason why both views have tracks that seem to be exactly the same is that they *are* exactly the same. Session View has a dual function as a mixer view and as a way of triggering clips in a nonlinear order, as opposed to the linear Arrangement View.

8. Try triggering some clips now by triggering what is known as a *scene*. You can do this by clicking the arrow corresponding to the scene you created in the previous step. Click the small arrow in the Master section of the Arrangement View, as shown in Figure 3.9.

Source Au ⊙	MIDI Bass	MIDI Drum ⊙	6 Glass Pian	7 Audio	8 Harmony t		Master	
☐	☐	☐	☐	☐	☐		▷	1
▨	▶MIDI 2 2-Au	▶MIDI 1 1-Au	▶	▶1 7-Audio	▶MIDI 1 7-Au		▶	21
☐	☐	☐	☐	☐	☐		▷	2
☐	☐	☐	☐	☐	☐		▷	3
☐	☐	☐	☐	☐	☐		▷	4

Figure 3.9 Triggering a scene in the Session View of Ableton Live.
Source: Ableton AG

I pointed out the Scene button before anything else in the previous step because if you get scenes, you get the rest of the "grid" that's right there in front of you. If you don't look at things from a "scene" viewpoint first, I think it can make the learning process a little longer. Think of scenes like you think of parts of a song: You have a first verse, a chorus, a second verse, and so on. Well, scenes can be these parts and can be triggered any time you want. For example, Scene 1 can be your intro, Scene 2 can be your verse, and Scene 3 can be your chorus. In fact, you can even relabel scene numbers to match these exact words you use when you're putting a song together. Let's try that now.

9. Click on the box you just triggered so that it is highlighted. It most likely has a number within the box. By default, the scene boxes are always numbered sequentially. Change the name of the box to match what you think this current scene of music's role would be in a song. For example, if you think this part would be a verse, name it a verse—or an intro or a chorus, whatever you think it is. To relabel the box, use the Command/Ctrl+R shortcut, as shown in Figure 3.10.

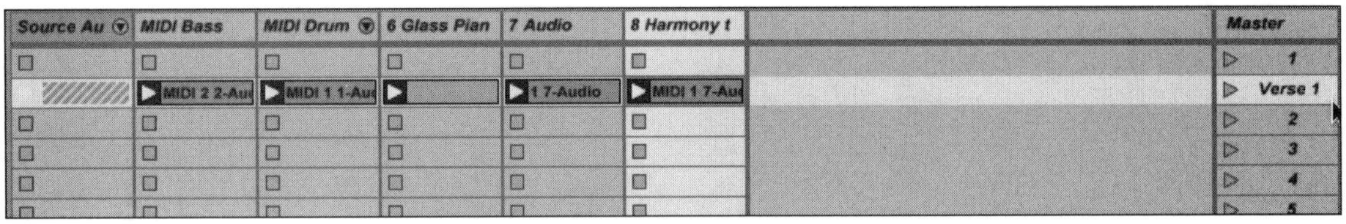

Figure 3.10 Renaming a scene in Session View.
Source: Ableton AG

10. Also, to prove that the Session View is as nonlinear as I claimed, I'd like to point out that you can also move scenes to different locations within the Session View. For example, if the scene you just labeled would be better suited as the very first scene in your song, you can move it up. Try this now: Drag the session up to where it becomes the very first scene in the Session View, as shown in Figure 3.11. You'll notice that my cursor has changed to denote that I'm moving something and that a bold line has appeared to reference where the final destination will be.

Being able to label and rearrange scenes and their order is an incredible way to create and reimagine the arrangement of a song. By simply breaking down parts of a song and grouping them, you can trigger them any way you want. Live even lets you record how you trigger them to create new arrangements. And, yes, we'll be getting to that soon.

Figure 3.11 Move a scene to a different location within the Session View.
Source: Ableton AG

11. Now that we've looked closely at scenes and you are beginning to get an understanding of how they work, let's take a look at individual clips within a scene. You'll notice that every clip (the little colored boxes) within the session has an arrow next to it, as did the scene box, or slot, that you triggered in Step 8. This is because you can actually trigger individual loops outside of a scene to build new parts and so on. Try triggering an individual clip, as I've done in Figure 3.12. One of the many cool things about this way of working is that you aren't really bound by the procedures that you've used with other music apps.

You can trigger scenes if you'd like, and the scene will trigger multiple clips, or you can trigger individual clips and just jam out. And, you can record your progress in both ways, as soon as you press the Record button in Session View. Try launching some individual clips, and then let's move on.

Figure 3.12 Trigger an individual clip in Session View.
Source: Ableton AG

12. If you'd like to stop a scene or a clip, simply press the Stop button found at the base of the column within the Session View. Stop buttons are small, square buttons that let you essentially "reset" what's currently active within a column. See Figure 3.13.

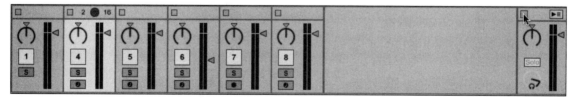

Figure 3.13 Stop a clip by using the column Stop button.
Source: Ableton AG

13. You can also copy clips to different scenes. This can be particularly helpful in building new parts of your song. For example, when you're creating a song, you know that you'll use many of the same drum grooves in different sections of the song. By having copies of different clips in different scenes, you can continually keep the groove going even though you're secretly switching to individual copies of the same loop. Let's try making a copy now. If you hold down the Option/Alt button and drag a clip down to a different slot, you'll notice that you're drag-copying the clip, as shown in Figure 3.14. Try copying a few different clips, but don't re-create the same group of clips in the next scene. Leave a few out. It can be even just one clip. Maybe this will be a break or something like that. Label the scene with whatever you think it should be. If you want, create a couple of scenes and label them.

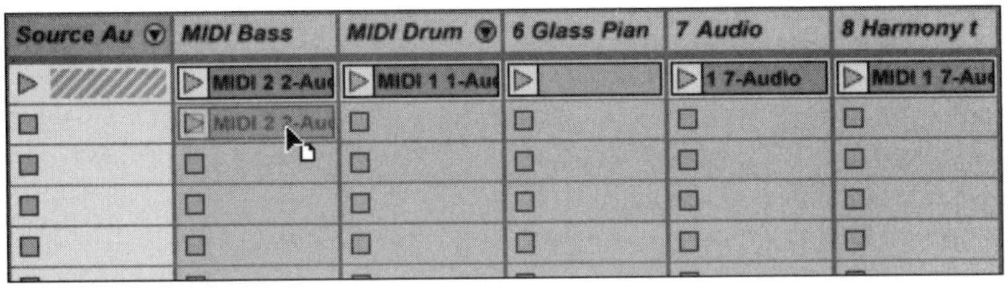

Figure 3.14 Copy a clip to a different scene in the Session View.
Source: Ableton AG

14. Now that you've got a few scenes in your Session View, let's see what all of the fuss is about. First, go back to the Arrangement View by pressing the Tab button and using the Command/Ctrl+A shortcut. This will, of course, select everything in the Arrangement View. Once everything is selected, press the Delete button to get rid of it. This isn't something you'd normally have to do; I'm just trying to prove a point here. Also, turn off Loop or Cycle mode! Once everything is deleted, go back to Session View and click the Arrangement Record button. Start triggering clips as you go along. You'll see the point in this later. Press the Stop button when you're finished. See Figure 3.15.

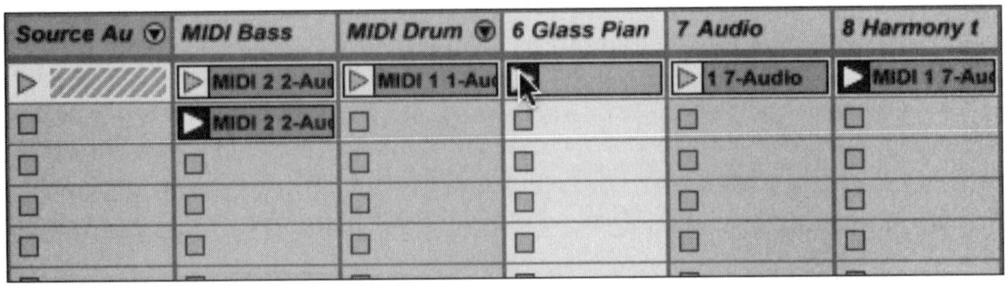

Figure 3.15 Recording in Session View.
Source: Ableton AG

15. Now, if you head back to the Arrangement View, you'll see a new array of clips that have all been positioned, coincidentally, in the manner in which you just played everything in Session View. You've just recorded an arrangement! Right now your head should be spinning, much like mine was after the first time I did this. You literally played conductor and arranged things the way you wanted the song to go. But the possibilities are far beyond this. Imagined triggering loops live, during a performance. You can extend the song far beyond normal sequencers, backing tracks, and so on. You could trigger loops at different times. You could even bring loops into your song that were never there before when you feel like it, instead of having to script this in as you would with a normal sequencer. In fact, you could actually have several parts of several songs within your Session View and run your entire set from Session View, triggering parts of different songs at random or doing mashups of your own songs.

16. But for the moment, let's return to the task at hand. You'll notice that the arrangement is currently grayed out. This means that although you recorded some excellent work, Live is still using the Session View clips as what will be played if you press the spacebar. However, if you press the small arrow button in the upper-right corner of the Arrangement View, you can put the focus back on what's in the Arrangement View. Press this button, shown in Figure 3.16, and listen to your work.

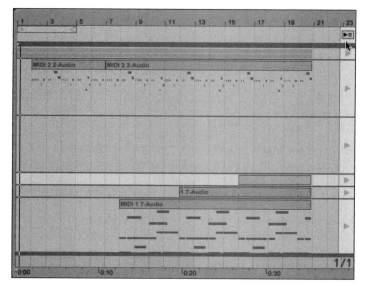

Figure 3.16 Pressing the Back to Arrangement button in the Arrangement View.
Source: Ableton AG

17. If you want to delete any sections that don't work for you, there are several options for editing. One extremely easy method for cleaning up your on-the-fly arrangements is to use the Delete Time function (see Figure 3.17). This literally truncates the entire section and bridges the gap for you, so that you don't have to drag things over. Try this now: Highlight a section of the song that you don't want and then use the Delete Time function in the Edit menu, or press Command/Ctrl+Shift+Delete. If you have multiple sections that you aren't happy with, feel free to use this command multiple times until you have everything the way you want it. However, I wouldn't spend too much time with it. We're going to be working more in the Session View for a while, and this is just an example arrangement.

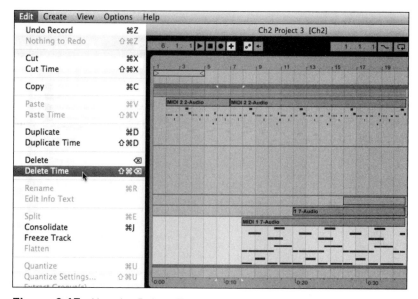

Figure 3.17 Use the Delete Time function in the Arrangement View.
Source: Ableton AG

All right, you've had your first encounter with Session View, something alien to most DAW users outside of Ableton. Hopefully, your head is reeling with new ideas for how you could utilize this very convenient and very creative resource for building songs, DJing, and building quick but intricate arrangements with just simple button presses.

Also, you're starting to see how the Session and Arrangement Views play into the overall Ableton production workflow. You'll notice that you can actually work exclusively in one view for the most part if you want. But as you get to know the whole Ableton system, you'll probably find yourself using all of it.

Now, let's take a look at the Session View for recording.

Recording in Session View

If you've ever used other loop-intensive applications, such as Vegas from Sony Creative Software, then you're probably familiar with simply slapping loops together that have been built from a loop library, and sometimes throwing your own vocals and so on over the top.

Although you can do this with Ableton, it was actually designed, since day one, to be an application that can quickly and easily create its own loops on the fly from your own recorded audio. And, while the loop method of recording tends to be frowned upon by some in the pro audio community, I highly recommend that you pay special attention to this section, as it can really change the way you engineer your recording sessions when working with talent and when doing things on your own with either your own voice or external instruments.

This method of recording changed the game for me. I used to give vocalists and instrumentalists some lead time before they would begin recording, so that they could hear the music and start to get into it, but as soon as I pressed the Stop button to go back for another pass, I could see the talent getting frustrated because they were already "in the moment" and could've just kept playing for minutes or maybe hours more...if I could've just kept the music going.

When I began tracking in Ableton, and once I became comfortable with the Session View, I began to enjoy the fact that I could keep the music going for long periods of time—and so did the talent that I worked with. Because I could keep looping music indefinitely, the talent had time to get into the music even more. I was able to pinpoint the takes where they were really into it—and even stack takes. But what was even better is that I could cue the performer, while the music was going, that I was going to trigger another part of the song, and I could even record a new take without them knowing. There's just a ton of flexibility!

So, for this next exercise, let's take a look at recording in Session View, using the method that I'm referring to—keeping the music going!

For this next exercise, I encourage you to use headphones if you are working on a laptop, because we will be recording vocals primarily. But if you have an external instrument you would like to record while you're singing, even better. Also, make sure that you start from where you left off in the previous exercise. You need something to build from, right?

1. Continuing from the previous exercise, create a new audio track and name it *Vox 1*. Make sure that the I-O section of the Ableton mixer column is visible in Session View.

2. Select the input you'll be using to record vocals. In my case, I'm using my built-in mic on my MacBook Pro. I like building up scratch vocals with this method in comfortable surroundings and then going back into the studio later and recording the vocals for real. If you're using a MacBook Pro like I am and you'd like to try this method, you might need to select the Configure option, also shown in Figure 3.18. This option will take you to the Audio page of the Live Preferences page. Here, you can select Built-in Mic, as opposed to Built-in Input. Once you've got a good signal coming in, make sure that you click the Record Arm button at the base of the mixer column.

Figure 3.18 Setting up inputs in the Ableton Session View.
Source: Ableton AG

3. Now that you have the inputs ready to go, cue the full scene that you brought in from the Arrangement View in the previous exercise (see Figure 3.19). Just let the music play and mentally prepare yourself to record some vocals. They can be scratch, and they don't need to be award-winning. This is just for the sake of learning!

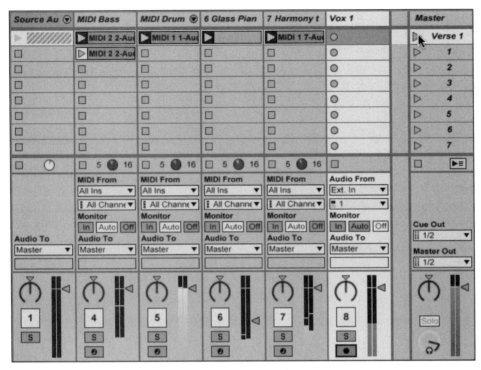

Figure 3.19 Playing a scene in the Ableton Session View.

Source: Ableton AG

4. When you are ready to begin recording your vocals, click the Record button in the clip slot adjacent to the other clips in your current scene. This will start audio recording for this clip slot, and audio waveforms will appear in the lower Clip View editor, as shown in Figure 3.20. Try to be aware of the clip's timing as you do this part of the exercise. As you get near the end of what you intend to record, click the Clip Launch button, which will look like a red arrow, again. This will cause Live to set the loop's loop point to the nearest solid measure. Do not press the spacebar at this point. Keep the music going!

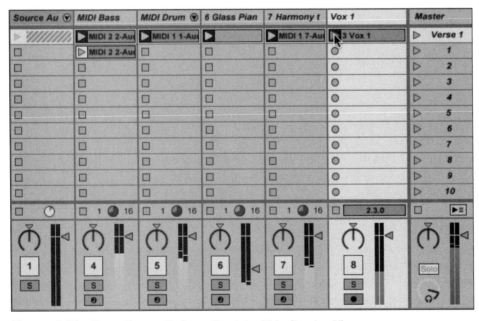

Figure 3.20 Recording audio in a clip slot within Session View.

Source: Ableton AG

5. Now that you have a clip of recorded audio, you probably want to edit the loop point. Even though I warned you about pressing the clip slot's Record button toward the end of your recording, it may still be off. This is something that you'll get used to over time. In fact, I still miss the loop points! As you can see in Figure 3.21, I seriously went over in my recording. What was supposed to be 4 measures is now 13 measures. I need to fix this. I'll move the loop end marker to Measure 5 and the loop start marker to what I think is the best start point. In most cases, you will not want to move your start marker, because this can throw off how the loop plays back in relation to the other parts. In my case, this is just a demonstration. When you've finished adjusting your loop points (if you even need to at all), proceed to the next step with the music still grooving on.

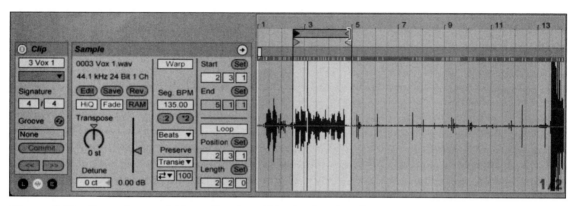

Figure 3.21 Recording audio in a clip slot within the Session View.
Source: Ableton AG

6. Now try this out for size. With the music still going, click the Record button for the clip directly underneath the clip slot you just used. Plan on singing, too! This is a great demonstration of how you can continue to create vocal takes on the fly while still keeping the mood, which is more important than people think. See Figure 3.22. In fact, repeat this step a few times. Get several takes together if you'd like.

Source Au	MIDI Bass	MIDI Drum	6 Glass Pian	7 Harmony t	Vox 1		Master
	▶ MIDI 2 2-Au	▶ MIDI 1 1-Au	▶	▶ MIDI 1 7-Au	▷ 3 Vox 1		▷ Verse 1
☐	▷ MIDI 2 2-Au	☐	☐	☐	▷ 4 Vox 1		▷ 1
☐	☐	☐	☐	☐	☐ 5 Vox 1		▷ 2
☐	☐	☐	☐	☐	○		▷ 3
☐	☐	☐	☐	☐	○		▷ 4
☐	☐	☐	☐	☐	○		▷ 5
☐	☐	☐	☐	☐	○		▷ 6
☐	☐	☐	☐	☐	○		▷ 7
☐	☐	☐	☐	☐	○		▷ 8
☐	☐	☐	☐	☐	○		▷ 9
☐	☐	☐	☐	☐	○		▷ 10
☐ ◖	☐ 2 ◕ 16	☐ 2 ◕ 16	☐ 2 ◕ 16	☐ 2 ◕ 16	☐ 2.1.0		☐ ▶≡
1	4	5	6	7	8		Solo
S	S	S	S	S	S		

Figure 3.22 Record additional takes while the music continues in the Session View.
Source: Ableton AG

7. While keeping the music going, you might consider creating an additional audio track (press Command/ Ctrl+T) and doing some vocal overdubs. But this time, instead of using the individual clip button, try using the Session Record button at the top of the screen. This button can be extremely handy, because it will cue as many clips as you have armed with the stroke of a button. This means that you can record multiple tracks within the Session View in perfect timing. Try using this button now to start recording. If you'd like to create multiple audio tracks and record arm several, Command/Ctrl-click on the Record Arm buttons to select multiple, as shown in Figure 3.23. When you're ready to stop the recordings, click the Session Record button again. You have just recorded several tracks at once and were able to cue them without ever stopping the music. C'mon now, you're starting to love Ableton, right?

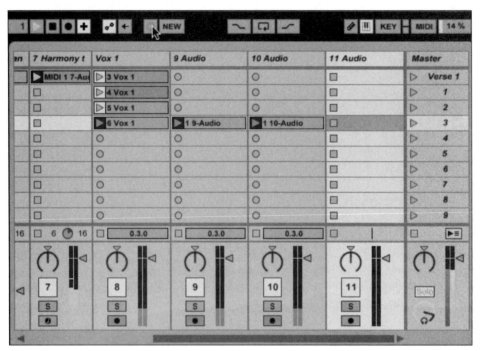

Figure 3.23 Cueing and recording multiple tracks at once in Session View.
Source: Ableton AG

8. Now that you've gotten your feet wet with Session View recording and you have several vocal takes under your belt, you should take a look at how to submix in Ableton. It's actually not that hard; it just requires the kind of bussing that you've already been doing, but in a slightly different way. Before you get started, group however many vocal tracks you created by Shift-clicking each track and using the Command/Ctrl+G shortcut to group your tracks. When your grouping is complete, you'll notice that every output on every track within your group actually says "Group." So, now you can apply effects to the Group track itself by simply dragging effects onto the Group track, as shown in Figure 3.24.

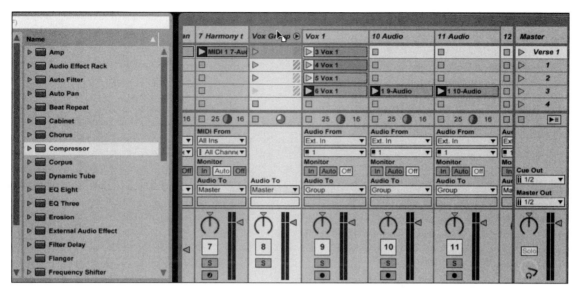

Figure 3.24 Dragging an effect from the Browser to a Group track in Session View.
Source: Ableton AG

So how was your transition to Session View? Is it everything you thought it would be? For me, it's a godsend. And once you're used to it, I think it will change things up for you, too.

It's important to remember that there really isn't a set way of doing anything in Session View. It's open-ended enough that you can really set up your own workflow. Don't feel as if anything you did in these exercises is the way that you *must* do things. They are just systems that I've enjoyed.

In the next chapter, we'll start getting into some stuff that is even more Ableton-specific. We're going to look at envelopes, how they work with plug-ins, and more.

See you there!

Session and Envelopes

N OW THAT YOU'RE FAMILIAR WITH RECORDING, BUSSING, GROUPING, and the Arrangement and Session Views in Ableton, it's time to start looking into some of the more subtle features in Ableton Live. While these aren't always the things that are talked about the most, I guarantee you that one of the features we will be covering in this chapter is one of the most widely used and beloved by serious Ableton Live users. Envelopes, which are available for both audio and MIDI clips, bring in some powerful automation features you won't find anywhere else.

Envelopes can help with sound sculpting, effects, or even very surgical work. You really won't believe how powerful they are. And after you've used them a bit, it will be hard to look back to your old DAW.

What Are Envelopes?

Let's take a look at this fascinating feature as I describe what takes place.

1. Double-click on a vocal track that you recorded from the previous exercise. This will cause the Clip View to appear at the bottom, as shown in Figure 4.1. Once you're in there, click the small E button, also shown in Figure 4.1.

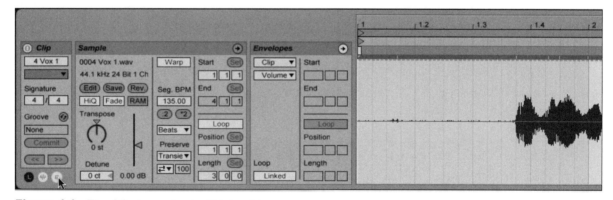

Figure 4.1 The Clip Inspector in Ableton Live.
Source: Ableton AG

You'll notice that as soon as you click the E button—which of course stands for *envelope*—you'll see a small editor appear with a couple of drop-down menus, shown in Figure 4.2. This box designates the parameters you are controlling with your envelopes at this moment. For example, in my clip, you'll notice that the upper drop-down menu says Clip and the drop-down menu below says Volume, short for Volume Modulation. This means if I draw in an envelope within the Clip editor, the volume of the clip will be affected. Let's try this out in the next step.

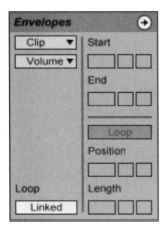

Figure 4.2 The Envelopes box in the Clip View of Ableton Live.
Source: Ableton AG

2. You'll notice that at the top of the Sample Editor, there is a very small pink dotted line. This line lets you know that there is currently no envelope automation on this particular parameter—that is, volume. Let's add some now. This clip has a lot of empty space at the front of it, and as a result, there's room noise. It could use a gate. But why not just cancel it out manually? Drag-select the empty area at the front, as shown in Figure 4.3. Before you go any further, by the way, make sure that you press the B button to toggle off Draw Mode. You'll know that Draw Mode is off if the small pencil button in the upper-right corner of the Live interface (not shown) is unlit.

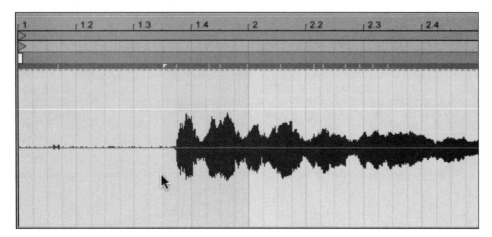

Figure 4.3 Drag-select part of an audio clip in the Envelope Editor of Ableton Live.
Source: Ableton AG

3. Now that you've selected a section of audio, it's really easy to tell Ableton where you want the envelope automation to begin and end. If you move your mouse slightly up toward the top of the clip, the dotted line will become solid, as shown in Figure 4.4. In fact, the whole audio waveform will change to a pinkish hue. Because this book is not in color, the pink may not be apparent in the picture, but you'll notice that the line at the top has become bold. And it's the bold line that we care about, anyway!

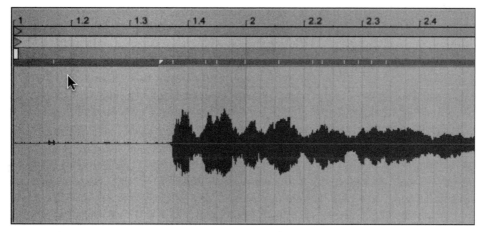

Figure 4.4 Moving toward the top of the audio waveform to see the envelope line appear.
Source: Ableton AG

4. As soon as the line becomes bold, click and drag down. This will cause the envelope adjustment to confine itself to the selected area only, as shown in Figure 4.5. Note: You don't need to actually touch the line; just drag down as soon as it becomes bold. In fact, drag the line all the way down to the bottom (not shown). You've just set up your first envelope!

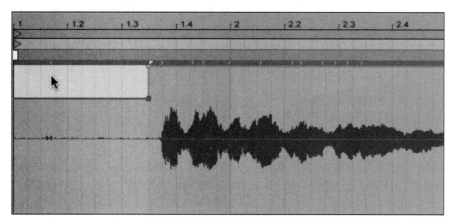

Figure 4.5 Modifying the clip/volume envelope in the Clip editor.
Source: Ableton AG

5. Now would be a good time to hear your handiwork, but because it's such a subtle adjustment, soloing would be the best call. Make sure that the M button for the mixer section is lit up, so that you can see your mixer controls, as shown in Figure 4.6. Realistically, you'd need this section available to record enable any of your tracks. But now it is time to pay more attention to this section. This is also where you'll start to see how the Session View becomes the main mixer for your Ableton Live project. Volume faders, Mute buttons, and Solo buttons are all here. There are even sends and returns, which you can toggle on and off separately. We'll get to the sends and returns later. For now, just click the Solo button that corresponds to the audio track for which you just adjusted the envelope. Just click the S button (not shown) that corresponds to the highlighted track in Session View.

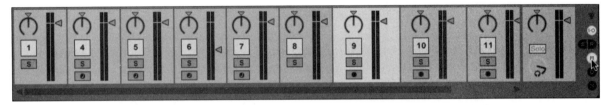

Figure 4.6 Enabling the mixer section in the Session View.
Source: Ableton AG

ENVELOPES ARE QUICK AND EASY: Nothing's more annoying than having to move around several parts of automation when you're in the middle of a project. This is especially true when you're scoring or you've just finished up a multi-parameter automation operation. This is where envelopes can really shine. Apply an envelope to a clip, and it will stay with the clip no matter how many times you copy it! Try it with panning, volume, MIDI parameters, and mixer functions.

6. Now that the track is soloed, you should be able to note where the envelope starts and stops as you listen to the looping of your audio track. Note: It doesn't have to be such a drastic cutoff. It can be sloped or even curve in. Let's try sloping first. You'll notice that toward the base of your envelope cutoff, there will be a small white dot. This is an envelope breakpoint (see Figure 4.7). When you hover over the breakpoint, it will tell you at the top what strength percentage this breakpoint represents, as shown in Figure 4.7.

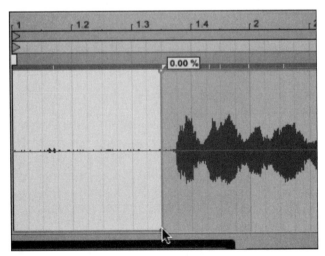

Figure 4.7 The Ableton Clip envelope breakpoint.
Source: Ableton AG

7. As with automation parameters in other DAWs, you can move around breakpoints so that Ableton knows how to fade in and fade out, and lets you adjust how things are going to work. Let's try moving the breakpoint so that the envelope fades in, as opposed to fading out. If you're using a breakpoint at the end of your audio waveform, as opposed to at the beginning, feel free to do this in reverse. In my case, I'll move the breakpoint to the very beginning of the waveform so that I get a gradual fade. See Figure 4.8.

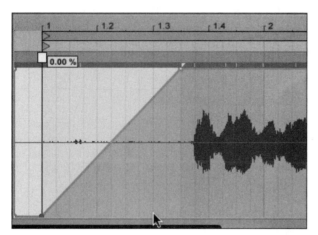

Figure 4.8 Creating an envelope fade-in.
Source: Ableton AG

8. Now that we have a gradual fade-in, what if we decide we want it to curve? In many DAWs, and in Live up until version 9, you would've had to create several breakpoints to achieve this. Not anymore, though! If you hold down the Option/Alt button near the sloping line, you'll notice that the cursor adds a small curved line next to it (not shown). Once you see this icon change, drag down while still holding the Option/Alt button. Your envelope section will bend, as shown in Figure 4.9.

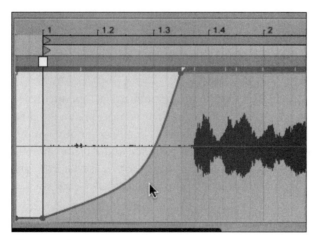

Figure 4.9 Curving an envelope in the Clip editor.
Source: Ableton AG

CURVES: Curves are also available in the regular automation in the Arrangement View. They're not just limited to envelopes!

---

9. If you run your cursor along the breakpoint envelope line, you'll notice that a pseudo-breakpoint will appear. In other words, Live will show you where the breakpoint could appear as you hover along. As soon as you're ready to create the actual breakpoint, just click. If you want to remove the breakpoint, simply click again. Try creating a few breakpoints for the fun of it, as shown in Figure 4.10.

While you're doing this, here are a few modifier keys to play with as you move along. If you hold down the Shift button while you drag a breakpoint, it will delete all other breakpoints along the envelope path. This can be handy for cleaning up your automation. If you hold down the Command/Ctrl button while moving a breakpoint, the movements will be far slower, so you can fine-tune the breakpoint settings in percentages and so on.

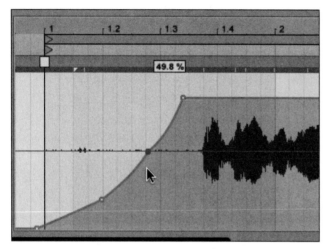

Figure 4.10 Create multiple breakpoints and modify them with modifier keys, such as Shift, Command/ Ctrl, and so on.
Source: Ableton AG

10. Let's try using an envelope on a different parameter now. Instead of using an envelope to automate clip/ volume modulation, let's try modulating the Ableton mixer and, in the process, see what else is available. To make the mixer your focal point, change the upper drop-down menu in the Envelopes section of the Clip Inspector to Mixer, as shown in Figure 4.11.

Once the mixer is your new target, the lower drop-down menu will have destinations for modulation such as Track Panning, Speaker On, and even access to your sends and returns, so that you can modulate them as well. Let's go with panning for the moment. This is actually one of my favorite modulation destinations since I began using Ableton. I love being able to create and hear complex stereo patterns, and Ableton allows you to get so intricate with the panning, so precise. It's really quite amazing. But the best part is that these intricate stereo patterns are contained specifically within a clip. They will loop with stereo intricacy each time a clip is triggered. No other DAW has this.

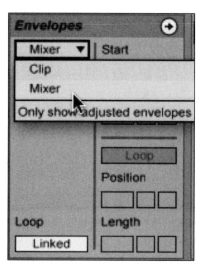

Figure 4.11 Select the mixer as the target for envelopes.
Source: Ableton AG

11. When you look at the default envelope setting for panning, you'll notice that it's a little different from the other envelopes, as shown in Figure 4.12. The default pink dotted line is in the middle of the clip, as opposed to at the top. This means that the higher you move the line, the more the panning is modulated to the right. The farther you move the line down, the more you modulate to the left. Try playing the clip soloed while you edit the panning envelope pattern.

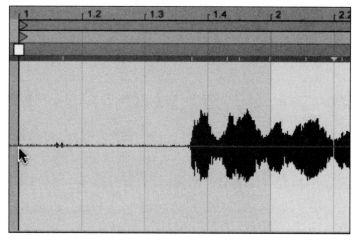

Figure 4.12 The default position for the panning envelope in the Clip editor.
Source: Ableton AG

12. While you're modulating the panning envelope, try adjusting your grid resolution using the Command/Ctrl+1 and 2 buttons. Using smaller grid sizes allows you to draw smaller, tighter patterns. Go tighter with the Command/Ctrl+2 shortcut. Or, you can go the opposite route by widening the grid lines using the Command/Ctrl+1 button, as shown in Figure 4.13. You can use either shortcut multiple times for wider or shorter grid lines.

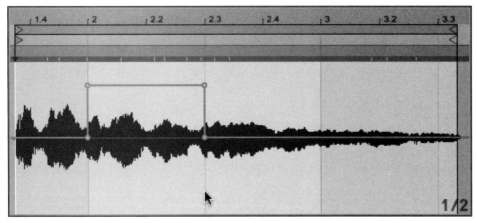

Figure 4.13 Wider gridlines in the Sample Editor section of the Clip editor.
Source: Ableton AG

13. As you edit your panning pattern, you may also consider switching in and out of Draw Mode using the B button. When you're in Draw Mode, click-dragging allows you to make fast, sweeping patterns, but in the resolution in which your grid is currently set. In Figure 4.14, notice that I made a quick, complex pattern, but it's in the resolution of my current grid. If I want a pattern with smaller, more intricate movements, I'll need to tighten my grid. If I want broader, more sweeping changes, I'll need to widen my grid when using the pencil. Try using Draw Mode now, while drawing in different grid resolutions.

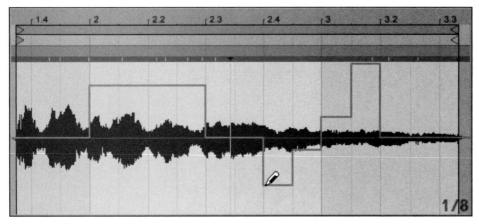

Figure 4.14 Use the Draw Mode to create quicker, more complex patterns.
Source: Ableton AG

14. When you have a pattern you like, press the B button again to switch out of Draw Mode. Look what happens! All of your work now has breakpoints. Now that the breakpoints are here, you can randomly select individual breakpoints that you don't like or simply remove a few to make smoother, less blocky panning transitions, as shown in Figure 4.15. Try holding down the Shift key to drag one breakpoint over other breakpoints so that they disappear. Try creating some smooth diagonal transitions.

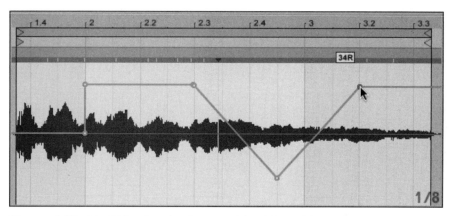

Figure 4.15 Modifying breakpoints outside of Draw Mode.
Source: Ableton AG

15. Remember, too, that you can zoom in to specific places in your sample, and the grid lines will adjust accordingly. If you move your cursor up to the top of the Sample Editor, the magnifying glass will appear, as shown in Figure 4.16. Once it's there, you can click and drag up or down to zoom into and out of your sample. I use this feature a lot because it gives me the opportunity to get some quick, tight, and precise panning transitions in. It is true that in the end, you may be the only person who notices this effect. But I guarantee that if you spotlight the transition well enough in your mix, people will ask you how you did it. And remember, this is an envelope—it loops like this all the time. It's extremely tight modulation that is here only for the loop/clip.

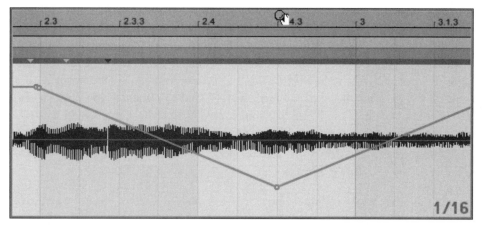

Figure 4.16 The magnifying glass at the top of the Sample Editor.
Source: Ableton AG

16. You may decide, for example, that you want the loop to pan left at the beginning of the first repetition and then pan right at the beginning of the second repetition. But you'll notice that there is room for automation to occur only once within the envelope. There is a way around this problem; it's solved by unlinking the envelope from the actual audio clip. By doing this, you make the envelope length independent of the clip length. You can do this by pressing the Loop Linked button in the Envelopes section of the Clip Inspector. As soon as it's

pressed, the button will toggle to Unlinked, as shown in Figure 4.17. The Loop section of the Envelopes section will become adjustable as well. Now, in the Length section, you can increase the looped length to four measures instead of two.

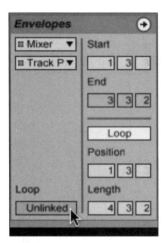

Figure 4.17 Unlink the envelope in the Envelopes box.
Source: Ableton AG

You'll notice that as soon as you go unlinked, the sample waveform will disappear. This occurs only for the unlinked envelope parameter, which in this case is panning. All other envelope targets will still be linked. So, when you switch back to clip volume, it will still show the waveform and be linked.

But what about the panning envelope setting? How can you edit without the waveform being visible? This can be the unfortunate downside of unlinking your envelopes. But the pros far outweigh the cons. To solve this, I generally create a complex pattern for the first two measures, or however long the actual audio loop is. Then, once I'm ready to expand the length of the envelope past the length of the audio loop, I copy the pattern that I created while linked to the measures that were added when I unlinked. You can do this easily by drag-selecting the envelope pattern and then using the Command/Ctrl+C and Command/Ctrl+V shortcuts. In fact, Ableton will actually move the highlighted area over to the next area, with the original length that you copied, with Command/Ctrl+V first, just to show you where it's going to move without pasting. Then, when you've confirmed that this is in fact your new targeted area, you can use the paste shortcut again to commit to the pasting procedure. It's quite cool. See Figure 4.18.

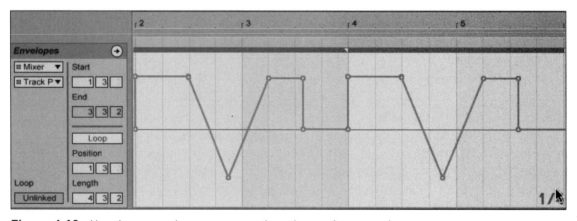

Figure 4.18 Use the paste shortcut to commit to the pasting procedure.
Source: Ableton AG

SELECTING AND PASTING WITH GRIDS: You may find it easier to adjust the grid resolution with the Command/Ctrl+1 and 2 shortcuts to get precise areas when selecting for copying and pasting. This is especially true for automation. By ensuring that you copy and paste on valid grid lines, you'll keep your automation in beat and ensure that you stay tight!

TIME IS NOT RELATIVE WHEN UNLINKING: The loop points in an unlinked envelope don't necessarily have to reflect the location where your audio actually occurs. In fact, you can increase and decrease the loop length or even move the loop point to a different location, past where the audio occurs. Try experimenting with this!

EXTERNAL PLUG-INS WORK, TOO: You'll be happy to know that all of the external plug-ins you run in Ableton Live can have envelopes triggering them, just like the internal Ableton devices and plug-ins. If you have a plug-in on your track, in the Envelopes section of the Clip editor choose the plug-in from the top drop-down menu, shown in Figure 4.19, to be your target. In the drop-down menu below, choose the parameter of your choice found on your plug-in or instrument. Note: Parameter lists on external plug-ins can be quite long. If you don't feel like rooting through the list to find the correct parameter, you might try the next exercise and use record automation instead.

Also, it's important to note that the parameter that you'd like to automate with an envelope may not appear until you move the knob during an automation recording session. Again, you learn to do this in the next exercise!

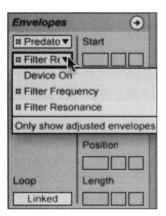

Figure 4.19 Choose an external plug-in as a target for an envelope.
Source: Ableton AG

Session View Automation

At this point you may be asking, "Do I have to manually draw all of my envelopes?" A few years ago, that would've been the case to some extent. But as of Ableton Live 9, this is no longer true. As of version 9, you can record knob movements, fader movements, and so on in real time, and your work will be laid down within the envelopes.

This is an extremely cool feature that makes music production fun and exciting in ways that other DAWs can't compete. For example, you can keep a section of a song going by triggering a scene. As this scene loops endlessly, simply record your automation tweaks as you would loop record with an old drum machine. When you feel it's dialed in, trigger the next scene. When all of your automation is to your liking in all of your scenes, record your arrangement into the Arrangement View and wrap it up.

In this next exercise, we'll focus on Session View automation: how to set it up, how linking and unlinking can expand the experience, and more.

If you want to save some of your envelope work from the previous exercise, I suggest saving your work. You could also create a new scene or two that you've marked specifically for recording automation. When you're ready, continue to the next exercise.

1. Choose a track in your Ableton Live session by clicking the Record Arm button on the selected track. If you want to record automation for more than one track, hold down the Command/Ctrl key and click the Record Arm button for each track you want to be active (see Figure 4.20). If you decide on a different track later, during the automation recording session, don't worry—you can enable other tracks during recording. Ableton is very forgiving!

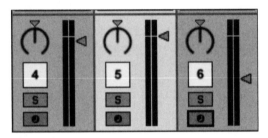

Figure 4.20 Record arm multiple tracks for automation.
Source: Ableton AG

2. Ensure that the Automation Arm button is enabled, as shown in Figure 4.21. When this button is active, in either the Session or Arrangement View, manual parameter changes will be recorded as long as recording is active.

Figure 4.21 Enable the Automation Arm button.
Source: Ableton AG

3. When you're ready, click the Session Record button, as shown in Figure 4.22. This will place into record mode all clips that are within the tracks that have been record armed. And note that if you press any keys during this operation, notes will be recorded in overdub mode if overdub mode is active, as shown in Figure 4.23. Either way, move faders, move pan knobs, and even double-click on the track titles to access the parameters of synths and other instruments you are using. Don't worry about messing anything up—you can undo this and start over if it doesn't work for you.

Figure 4.22 Click the Session Record button to begin automation recording.
Source: Ableton AG

Figure 4.23 The MIDI Arrangement Overdub button.
Source: Ableton AG

4. As you get toward the end of each clip, let the music continue to play and listen to your automation work. Is there anything you'd like to add? Would you like your automation pass of each parameter to be longer? If longer is the case, remember that you can go into the Envelope Editor section of the Clip editor and unlink to have a longer pass—even while the recording is active. See Figure 4.24.

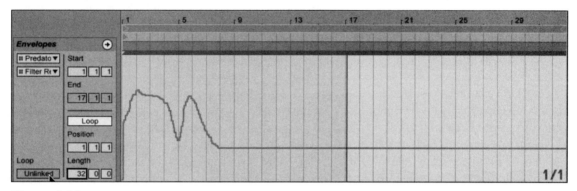

Figure 4.24 Unlink an envelope to extend automation record time.
Source: Ableton AG

5. When you've finished your automation recording session, click the Session Record button again—the same button you used to start automation recording. This will take you out of record mode, but you'll continue looping. From here, you can decide whether there's anything else you'd like to add. One interesting thing is that if you adjust a parameter that you've automated outside of record mode, the Re-Enable Automation button, shown in Figure 4.25, will light up to let you know that some of your work has been tweaked, and some of your automation is no longer active. To return automation to normal, just click the Re-Enable Automation button.

Figure 4.25 The Re-Enable Automation button.
Source: Ableton AG

6. If you elect to continue recording automation to different scenes, don't worry! No additional setup is required once record automation is in session. Just trigger the next scene and continue to do your fader sweeps, pan movements, and so on. And feel free to arm additional tracks and disarm tracks you no longer need.

As you can see, the Session View is mega-powerful. But with automation and envelopes, it's a pure music beast. And it can make extremely intricate automation passes seem like child's play. But it gets even better!

When you start adding in third-party plug-ins, you begin to see instruments you've used for a long, long time in a different light.

Virtual Instruments with Session View Automation

When you're using virtual instruments from a third-party source with Ableton Live with the intention of automation, you should know about a few features and tricks before moving forward.

As I noted earlier in this chapter, often parameters you'd like to automate may not be readily available within the target list in the Envelope Editor. And, as I mentioned, this is no big deal. You can simply move the knob or whatnot within the Virtual Instruments interface, and all is well. But how do you even access your third-party plug-in interface in Ableton Live?

In this next exercise, we'll take a closer look at setting up plug-ins, accessing their interfaces, and giving Ableton access to their individual parameters for better handling on your end.

1. Locate the Plug-Ins category in the Live Browser. This is where all of your AU and VST plug-ins are located, as shown in Figure 4.26. If you're on a Mac, you'll have two folders to switch between. In some cases, a manufacturer may make only a VST version of a plug-in. In other cases, a company may make only an AU version. If you're on a PC, you only have to worry about VST. Choose an instrument or an effect plug-in and assign either type to a track by dragging it from the Browser or by double-clicking. Note: If you double-click an instrument plug-in and an instrument track is selected, the instrument will replace the instrument currently on that track. If no track is selected, a new track will appear with the double-clicked instrument plug-in. When you have any sort of plug-in on any sort of MIDI or audio track, proceed to the next step.

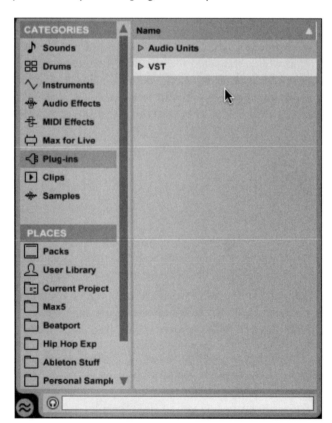

Figure 4.26 The Plug-Ins category of the Ableton Browser.
Source: Ableton AG

2. When either an effect or an instrument is created in a track, a device enclosure of sorts will appear. This device technically holds your VST or AU plug-ins in it. It also sports a couple of handy features that make working with your plug-in in Live much cooler. The most obvious feature is the XY pad, highlighted in Figure 4.27, that appears in the center of the device. You can assign individual plug-in parameters to the X- and Y-axes, which will allow you to easily morph between different settings. This is especially handy if you're just jamming out on a laptop and you don't have access to a controller. Currently, you don't have any options available to assign to the XY pad. In fact, you don't even know how to access the main plug-in interface yet. Let's look at how to do this.

Figure 4.27 The XY pad.
Source: Ableton AG

3. In the upper-left corner of the device enclosure, you'll notice a little wrench symbol, as shown in Figure 4.28. This button, the Plug-In Edit button, exposes the actual plug-in interface in Ableton Live. Click this button so that you can fully navigate the device you're working with.

Figure 4.28 The Plug-In Edit button.
Source: Ableton AG

4. Once your plug-in is shown visibly in the way that you are accustomed to, click the small Unfold Device Parameters button, next to the Plug-In Edit button. This button allows you to access various parameters for the third-party plug-in you're working with inside Ableton Live, without having to open up the device itself. Currently, no parameters are shown because you haven't configured anything yet (see Figure 4.29).

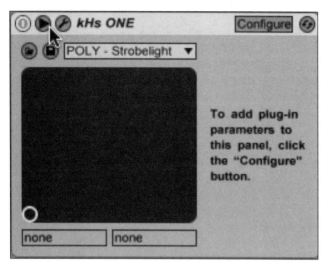

Figure 4.29 Click the Unfold Device Parameters button.
Source: Ableton AG

5. Click the Configure button at the top of the device enclosure and start pushing buttons and moving sliders in your third-party plug-in. Notice how they start to appear within the Ableton device enclosure now, as shown in Figure 4.30.

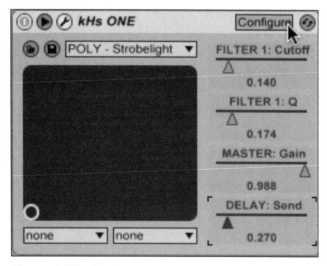

Figure 4.30 Configure third-party device parameters in Ableton Live.
Source: Ableton AG

6. Now that these parameters are available in Live, assign some to the XY pad. By doing this, you'll have much easier control when you aren't using a MIDI controller. And it's easier to actually "see" what is taking place, because the XY pad will visually move after it has been automated. Assign parameters by using the drop-down menus at the bottom of the device enclosure, as shown in Figure 4.31. The left drop-down menu is X, and the right is Y. Assign parameters to the X and Y now.

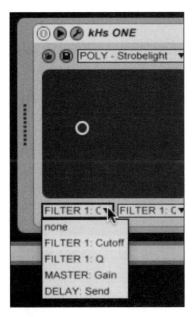

Figure 4.31 Assign third-party parameters to the XY pad in Live.
Source: Ableton AG

7. Now try recording some automation with the XY pad. Just move the little ball around. Notice how fun and easy it is to just move the ball up and down and hear amazing results. Note: You can also change X or Y assignments, even during recording, and start triggering other parameters whenever you want. By overdubbing, you can get some seriously wicked automation tweaks. Notice that as soon as you start recording automation with the XY pad, whatever parameters you have assigned will turn red. This indicates that these parameters are now being automated, as shown in Figure 4.32.

Figure 4.32 Automated parameters in the device enclosure of Ableton Live.
Source: Ableton AG

It's extremely easy to use third-party plug-ins in Ableton Live 9. But it goes beyond that. Because so much thought and attention has been put into Live with regard to how to make third-party plug-ins, you may find yourself doing things with your synths and effects that you may have never thought of before.

As we move forward, we'll continue to work with both internal and external plug-ins as we begin learning more about the Live mixer.

5

Mix and Effects

A s I've mentioned, the closest thing to a real mixer in Ableton Live is the Session View interface. After all, it lines up audio and MIDI tracks side by side, like channels on a mixing board. These channels also have pan, volume, and input controls. Of course, you can't see the inserts; they are hidden and require a double-tap on the label of the channel for you to see the inserts that are assigned at the bottom of the screen.

Thankfully, this mixing console style of view does—and will always, I hope—exist in Live, because it's the only familiar, visual systems in Live, like the Arrangement View with its familiar lanes. And because this portion of Live is laid out in a "classic" manner, it can be easy to understand.

In this chapter, we'll focus strongly on mixing as it exists in Ableton Live. We'll also explore effects and options, such as send and return tracks. We'll even take a look at effect Racks.

We'll start by simply seeing what is available for mixing within the Session View. You'll get a lay of the land, so to speak.

Mixer Anatomy in the Session View

Not all elements of the Session View's mixing capabilities are always in view. This is a good thing, because the screen can get pretty cluttered if you aren't careful. But Live does have a good system for ensuring that there is some ongoing organization.

Let's explore a bit of this mixer anatomy by first getting to know Live's send and return tracks.

1. In your ongoing project, you have a fair bit going on now. You've got a vocal group, some instruments, and so on. Because CPU processing power is a valuable commodity, and good effects tend to eat up a lot of that power, let's look at a great way to maximize your effects and build an environment. Sends and returns in Live work just as you're accustomed to in other DAWs, but in my opinion they offer a lot of flexibility. To enable or disable viewing of returns, click the Show/Hide Returns button, shown in Figure 5.1.

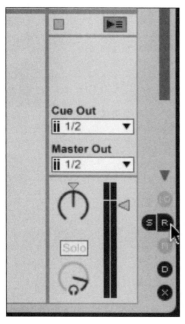

Figure 5.1 The Show/Hide Returns button as it appears in the Live Session View.
Source: Ableton AG

2. Return tracks hold effects just like regular tracks. However, it is important to note that return tracks cannot hold audio or MIDI clips. So, if you'd like to set up a return track with an insert effect that can be shared over multiple tracks through the sends, simply drag an effect onto the return track of your choice. Let's try adding one of Live's native effects. Click the Audio Effects category in the Live Browser and then locate the Reverb effect (see Figure 5.2).

Figure 5.2 The Audio Effects category in the Live Browser.
Source: Ableton AG

3. Drag the Reverb from the Browser onto Return Track 1. Nothing will happen visually, but you'll notice that the return track's title will instantly be labeled "A Reverb," as shown in Figure 5.3. And, of course, you'll want to be able to edit the reverb that you've incorporated into your project. If you double-click on the A Reverb title, as it appears at the top of the Session View, the reverb will suddenly become visible in the Device View.

Figure 5.3 The track title bar in Ableton Live.
Source: Ableton AG

4. Now let's actually hear the reverb. Because it's set up to be a return, you'll need to send to the return to hear anything. Thankfully, you have a few tracks ready to go. Use the vocal group you set up earlier. To raise the send level, though, you need to be able to see the send. Next to the Show/Hide button you used earlier to access the returns, locate the S button next to the R button you used to show the returns. Click this button, if it's not already lit up. See Figure 5.4.

Figure 5.4 The Show/Hide Sends button.
Source: Ableton AG

5. With the sends now shown, raise Send A on the Vocal Group main track until the reverb is playing at a level that is suitable to you and your vocals, as shown in Figure 5.5. As you can see, the sends and returns work in a very straightforward fashion. But you'll be happy to know that they are highly flexible in their use, much like a real analog board is. As we continue, I'll show you what I mean.

Figure 5.5 Raise Send A in Ableton Live's Session View.
Source: Ableton AG

6. Now that you have a reverb set up, you'll add in another classic effect—a chorus. Locate Chorus in the Audio Effects category of the Browser. Let's set up this effect on Return B. Just follow the same procedures from the previous couple of steps or refer to Figure 5.6.

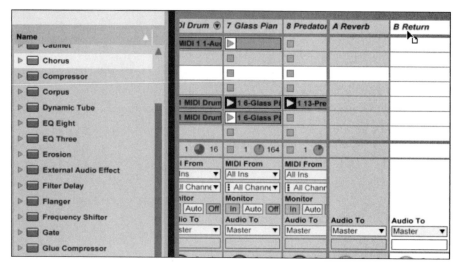

Figure 5.6 Set up Return B.
Source: Ableton AG

7. As you can see, working with the sends and returns is fairly simple. But let's take a look at some other capabilities of working with them. First, you should be aware that you aren't limited to only two returns. Use the Command+Option+T (PC: Ctrl+Alt+T) shortcut to create an additional return (see Figure 5.7). Up to 12 return tracks can be created in a Set.

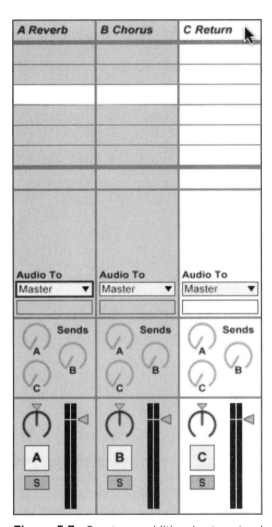

Figure 5.7 Create an additional return track.
Source: Ableton AG

8. As on all pro mixing boards, you can use return tracks and sends for additional purposes aside from effects tracks. I've had great success in using Ableton to set up discrete mixes for live performances. This includes setting up click tracks, choosing what instruments will be heard in each performer's headset or monitors, and so on. Achieving this all stems from setting the audio outputs of return tracks to external audio outputs. You can do this by setting the Audio To drop-down menu to Ext. Out and then selecting the output on your audio interface that has the end-result headset or monitor connected (see Figure 5.8). Try this now if you have an audio interface with multiple outs connected.

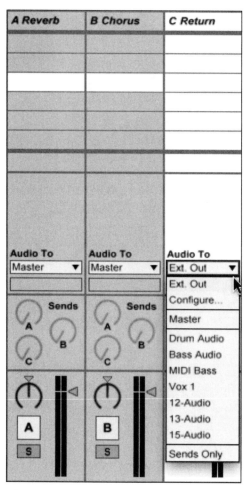

Figure 5.8 Set the output of the return track.
Source: Ableton AG

> **CLICK TRACKS FROM ABLETON LIVE:** As I mentioned, it's possible to send discrete submixes from Ableton to other performers for live performance and just for comfort in the studio. In doing this, you'll probably run into a situation where you want a click track to send to a drummer, and so on. A great way to do this is to record a metronome and then use it as a loop in either the Session or the Arrangement View. To keep the metronome from being heard on the main mix, set the metronome track (that you create) output to Sends Only. Then raise the send on the metronome track so that it goes to the return track of your choice. The return track will be set to the monitor, headphone, or in-ear monitor of the performer who needs to hear the click track. Problem solved!

9. Also notice the Pre/Post toggle on the master output for sends. This feature can be cool for a number of reasons, but the main one is the ability to choose whether you want to submix to an external output using the sends or rely on the pan and fader settings of tracks sending to the return track. Especially in the case of reverb return tracks, I've found that it's very easy to get a ghostly quality by lowering my fader all the way down on a pad track, for example, switching the send going to the reverb to Pre, and then sending a slight amount of signal with the send to the return track. Try this with a track of your own. Turn the track volume all the way down with the fader for the track. Then, send a small amount of signal to your reverb return. Finally, set the sends on the master channel to Pre, as shown in Figure 5.9.

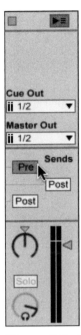

Figure 5.9 The Pre/Post toggles on the Master track.

Source: Ableton AG

10. It's also important to note that you can create some very cool feedback with return channels. If you notice, there are also Sends knobs on the return tracks themselves. These knobs are grayed out by default, but you can enable them. If you right-click on the Sends and choose Enable Send, the send will become active. See Figure 5.10. If you raise the send while the signal is being sent in from another channel, you may get some really cool feedback. Just be careful!

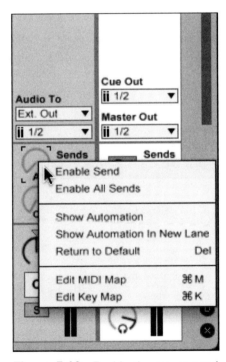

Figure 5.10 Enable the return send.

Source: Ableton AG

11. While you're customizing and creating sends and returns, I'd like to show you a few more tricks with the mixer, just to make you feel more at home. One extremely valuable feature in Live is the ability to customize the current views based on what you're doing. You can even move parts around. One helpful customization when you're mixing is to increase the length and width of your tracks within the Session View. This makes the tracks look and behave much more like a regular mixer. Try this out: Move your cursor to the seam of a particular track's title, within the title bar. The cursor will change to a [. Now, with this cursor variation in place, drag the seam over so that the width of your track changes, as shown in Figure 5.11.

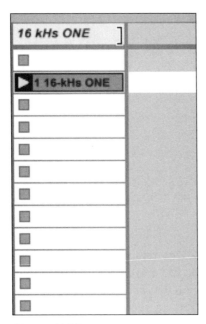

Figure 5.11 Increase the width of a track in Session View.
Source: Ableton AG

12. You can increase the length of the mixer section in a very similar fashion. Move your cursor to the top edge of the mixer section and then drag up. Suddenly, decibel points will appear, as you would see on a hardware mixer. See Figure 5.12. This can be extremely helpful if you're used to having visual indicators as you mix.

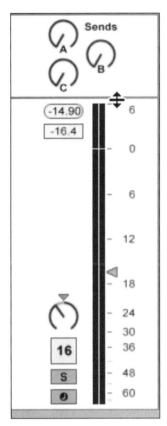

Figure 5.12 Increase the height of the mixer section.
Source: Ableton AG

Okay, that's a good amount of basic mixer anatomy for the moment. With Live's elasticity and its ability to modify itself to suit many needs, it's easy to see why so many people have moved to it as a one-stop shop. And with its flexibility in terms of sends, returns, and routing in its mixer, you are probably starting to hear and see how you can modify and maximize your Ableton sound.

Now let's move on to some more effects information, but in a slightly different way.

Effect Racks

Now that you're beginning to explore mixing and effects in Ableton Live, it's important to show you ways to keep your sessions not only organized, but also more tweakable.

The Audio Effect Rack does both. By giving you a container device, it makes it possible to merge several effects so that you don't have to toggle through many different devices. And, by giving you the effect Rack programmer, you're able to modify the roles of each effect within your effect Rack and get possibilities that you wouldn't be able to achieve outside of a Rack. Let's start looking at effect Racks and how they can assist you in getting some killer sound.

1. Currently, you have a Reverb on Return A and a Chorus on Return B. Drag the Chorus from Return B so that it also sits on Return A. This unto itself is a good lesson, because you're suddenly aware of the fact that the returns can host more than one effect. But we're going to take this much further. See Figure 5.13.

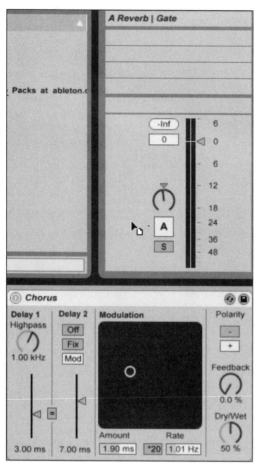

Figure 5.13 Move an effect from one return to another.

Source: Ableton AG

2. Now that the Chorus and the Reverb are both sitting in the same return, merge them into an Audio Effect Rack. To do this, click on the Reverb's title bar in the Device View at the bottom. Then, hold the Shift button and select the Chorus. The title bars for both devices will be highlighted. When you've done this, right-click and select Group. See Figure 5.14.

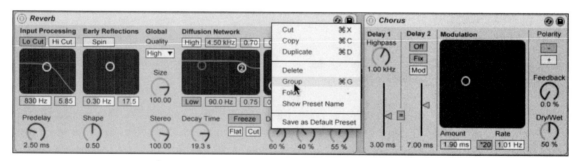

Figure 5.14 Group two effects devices.

Source: Ableton AG

> **THE POWER OF GROUPING:** Though it may not seem like it at first, grouping devices to create Racks in Ableton is a powerful way of creating new effects devices from existing devices. But it goes much further than mere blending. Using macros, you can map specific functions to particular macro knobs you use frequently. This can ultimately lead to new and exciting ways to morph, bend, and distort, which can be even more powerful when you get into creating Instrument Racks and Drum Racks, because creating each effect Rack is kind of like making an environment of your own to go. You'll ultimately find yourself gravitating back to custom Racks you've made, because they are effects environments that come straight from your own set of preferences.

3. Although it may not look like it now, the two devices are grouped. The only initial distinguishing difference is the new brackets on both sides. Also, on the far left you'll notice some buttons. These actually open up the more powerful portions of the effect Rack you just made. You can activate one of these portions by clicking the top button underneath the regularly seen Power buttons for each device in Live. Click the Show/Hide Macro button. See Figure 5.15.

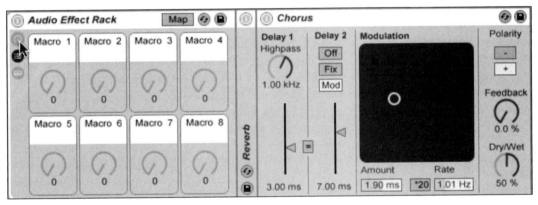

Figure 5.15 Click the Show/Hide Macro button.
Source: Ableton AG

4. As they exist in effect, Instrument, and Drum Racks, macros serve multiple purposes. Or, more specifically, they serve any purpose you'd like them to. Assigning a device parameter to be controlled by a macro is extremely easy. Simply right-click on the parameter you'd like to assign and then choose which macro it should go to from the contextual menu. Let's try this now. Right-click on the Reverb's Dry/Wet knob and choose Macro 1 from the contextual menu, as shown in Figure 5.16. Once assigned, you'll notice that a green dot appears next to the assigned knob. This lets you know that this function is already assigned within a Rack map.

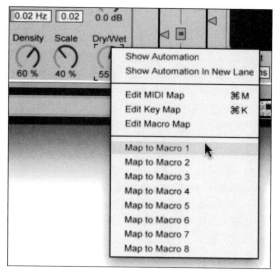

Figure 5.16 Assign a Dry/Wet knob to a macro.
Source: Ableton AG

5. Another way to map within the Racks is through the Map mode. By pressing Map in the Rack Editor front end, shown in Figure 5.17, you can access this mode. Once pressed, all of the mappable parameters within your group of effects will turn green. If you simply click on one of these parameters, you'll notice that the small Map buttons that appear under the Macro knobs will become bold, letting you know that you can press them. In my opinion, using this mode can greatly speed up the Rack-creation process, simply because all of your options are suddenly highlighted. And the options that are no longer available have small indicators letting you know they are already assigned. There's no guessing. In the Map mode, click the Feedback on the Chorus knob and then press the Macro 2 Map button. This will assign the Feedback knob to Macro 2.

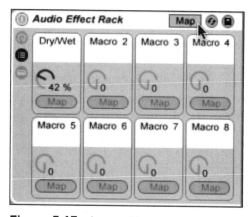

Figure 5.17 Access Map mode by pressing Map in the Rack Editor front end.
Source: Ableton AG

NAVIGATING THROUGH THE EDITOR: If you're having a hard time figuring out how to move through all the effects that you currently have assigned as an insert, send, and so on, try this out. When you're in the Device View, a small graphic appears at the bottom of Ableton. It shows you all the instruments currently in this editor (see Figure 5.18). You can click and drag on this graphic, and it will move you through the chain of devices that you currently have assigned. This makes it easy to program and tweak everything. This is known as the Device View selector.

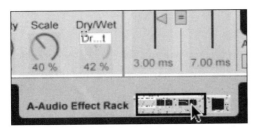

Figure 5.18 Scroll through effects with the Device View selector.

Source: Ableton AG

6. Another matter of great interest is the fact that you can actually map more than one parameter to one macro. Let's explore this now. While still in Map mode, click the Freeze button on your reverb. Then click the Map button on Macro 2. Now you have the chorus feedback and the Freeze button assigned to Macro 2. Because this macro is doing more than one function now, it might be a good idea to give it a new name. I'm going to rename my macro *Mangler*; try a name that you feel best describes what you've created. Use the Command/Ctrl+R shortcut to rename the label, as shown in Figure 5.19.

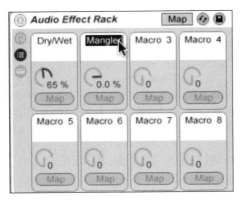

Figure 5.19 Rename a macro.

Source: Ableton AG

7. While in Map mode, you've probably noticed that the Mapping Browser has temporarily replaced the regular Live Browser. With the Mapping Browser, you can modify the macros that you've already created to suit your purposes. For example, the parameters that you assign to a macro don't necessarily have to function the way they normally do on their respective devices. You can modify the polarity of the macro so that it moves the knob the opposite direction. Truly, it's a way to make your own devices out of the many within Ableton Live. To see what I mean, try this: Change the minimum of the Mangler (Freeze On) to 127 and then set the Max to 64. Now if you try the Mangler knob, you'll have turned the Freeze of the Reverb on when the Mangler knob is all the way down. But with the way things are set up, if you raise the knob, the Chorus feedback will cause some crazy modulation (see Figure 5.20).

Macro	Path	Name	Min	Max
Dry/Wet	Chain | Reverb	Dry/Wet	0.0 %	100 %
Mangler	Chain | Reverb	Freeze On	127	64
Mangler	Chain | Chorus	Feedback	0.0 %	95 %

Figure 5.20 The Mapping Browser.
Source: Ableton AG

8. I bet the light bulb is going off over your head now, eh? Racks are very powerful! But the rabbit hole goes much deeper. Within the Audio Effect Rack, there's also another extremely cool feature. The button underneath the Show/Hide Macro button, on the left side of the Rack, will allow you to see another very handy section of the Rack—the Chain List. Click this button, as shown in Figure 5.21.

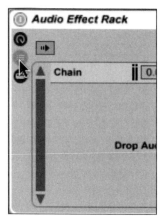

Figure 5.21 Click the Show/Hide Chain List button.
Source: Ableton AG

9. Chains are an extremely interesting component of the Rack environment. This is true for effects, instruments, and drums. Essentially, they allow you to have multiple Racks within a Rack and allow you to chain specific devices within a Rack for specific purposes. This is a little tricky to understand at first, but we'll go through it together. I can assure you that once you understand chains, you'll be more than gratified. Currently, you'll notice that in the Chain List, we have one chain. If you click on this chain, it will be two effects devices that you already know about—the Reverb and the Chorus. But if you drag another effect into the Chain List, something really curious will happen. Try this now: From the Browser, drag a simple delay onto the gray area that says "Drop Audio Effects Here," as shown in Figure 5.22. Do not drop the simple delay on the existing chain!

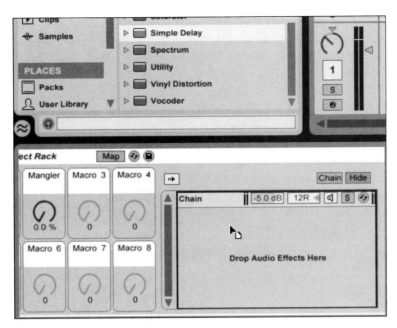

Figure 5.22 Drop Audio Effects Here.
Source: Ableton AG

10. Within your blooming Audio Effect Rack, you now have two chains holding three different devices. But only two devices are on one chain—the first two. The delay is on the second chain if the previous step was done correctly. Try selecting between the different chains to see what I'm talking about.

11. Because you're starting to build up multiple devices, you should probably label your chains. I'm going to label my first chain *RVB-Chr*. My second chain will be *Delay*, as shown in Figure 5.23.

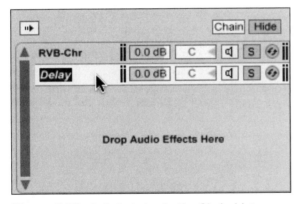

Figure 5.23 Label chains in the Chain List.
Source: Ableton AG

12. You'll notice on the chains themselves that you can also adjust the signal strength of the device's output and the panning of the device. There's even an activation button to bring the device into and out of play, as well as a Hot Swap button you can use to swap devices into and out of chains on the fly, through the use of the Browser. And while these are some great functions, there are more that give an even greater impression of what the effects can do. Let's take a look at this now. Click the Chain button at the top of the Chain List, next to the Hide button.

13. Welcome to the Zone Editor, a truly amazing piece of engineering. Zones allow you to determine, on the fly, which effects within each chain will be active. For example, you may want to be able to have the delay work some of the time and have the reverb and chorus work separately at other times. And, you may want all three effects to work together sometimes. The Zone Editor helps you set up how and when they work. You can see how this works by setting up a zone. The zones themselves are blue ranges that can be extended from the Chain List. They initially appear as blue blocks, but if you hover your cursor near them, you'll notice that you can extend them. Try dragging a zone from the RVB-Chr chain all the way to 32. Then drag the Delay chain's zone so that it starts at 16 and ends at 48. This means that the reverb and chorus will work by default, but the delay will need a little help to come into audible range. See Figure 5.24.

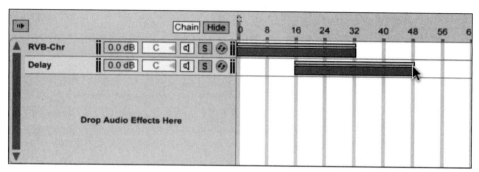

Figure 5.24 Edit zones in the Zone Editor.
Source: Ableton AG

14. The number values that you were dragging to and from in the Zone Editor only represent MIDI values. Essentially, they are just a measurement system to define parameters. What's important is to see what you've accomplished. At the very top of the Zone Editor, you'll see a small orange line. This is the Chain selector. If you drag this orange line around while your song is playing, you'll notice that if you're within a zone that has only Reverb and Chorus, you'll hear only these effects. If you're in an area where the zones overlap, you'll hear all effects. And if you're within an area where only the Delay zone is present...well, you'll hear only delay. This is where you begin to see the real power of the Audio Effect Rack—you can set up multiple effects that you can blend or activate separately. It's even possible to set up the Zone selector to be controlled by a macro. Try this: Click the Map button and then select the Zone selector (the orange line). When it's selected, click the Map button on Macro 3 to map the Zone selector to this macro. See Figure 5.25.

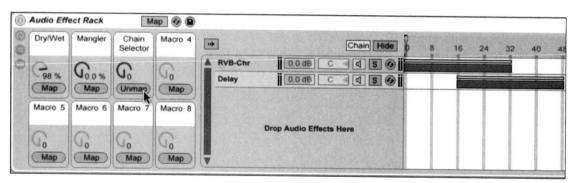

Figure 5.25 Map the Zone selector.
Source: Ableton AG

15. You'll notice that if you move the Zone selector around, you can now employ separate effects at will or blend them. But you'll also notice that if you move the macro too far over, there's no effect at all. This is because the zones have only a certain signal range based on how we set them up. Thankfully, Ableton's mapping system will allow you to curb the range of the macro so that it stops where you want it to. Bring up the Map Editor and then adjust the Max strength value of the Chain Selector so that it ends at 48, as shown in Figure 5.26. When you leave Map mode, you'll notice that there's always an effect going on. You can never move too far out.

Macro	Path	Name	Min	Max
Chain Selector		Chain Selector	0	48
Dry/Wet	RVB-Chr | Reverb	Dry/Wet	0.0 %	100 %
Mangler	RVB-Chr | Reverb	Freeze On	127	64
Mangler	RVB-Chr | Chorus	Feedback	0.0 %	95 %

Figure 5.26 Modify the Zone selector map values.
Source: Ableton AG

16. Finally, let's make it so the two effects zones can blend more seamlessly into one another. After all, wouldn't it be nice to have a little bit of delay on top of the Reverb, as opposed to all of it? Above the blue zone sections, you'll notice a lighter blue line. If you hover directly next to the light blue line, it will light up, letting you know that you can move it independent of the dark blue line. This light blue line signifies the fade range, and this is your means of creating gradual fade-ins and fade-outs of effects. Make your fade ranges match the ones shown in Figure 5.27. The Reverb and Chorus come in light and then build, and as the Chain selector moves farther along, it gradually fades in some delay. At the end of the Chain selector range, it's only delay. Cool, eh?

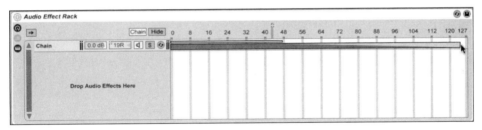

Figure 5.27 Fade effects in the Zone Editor.
Source: Ableton AG

And there you have it—you've begun building your first piece of Ableton kit. Even with its modest beginnings, it's a pretty sophisticated piece of gear. And there's so much more you can do. In the next chapter, we're going to move even further into Racks with drums and instruments.

Make sure you save at this point, and we'll continue on from here in the next chapter.

6

Instrument Racks

FOLLOWING THE INTRODUCTION OF RACKS IN THE PREVIOUS CHAPTER, I'm sure you're chomping at the bit to find out more about combining devices. As luck would have it, that's what this chapter is all about: Racks.

In this chapter, you'll get to know the Instrument Rack.

Instrument Rack

We haven't really taken a look at the individual instruments of Ableton Live yet, and that's okay. Actually, by building an Instrument Rack, you can get a really good understanding of the some of the smaller components and learn how they can be combined and tweaked to make an even bigger instrument. But why would you do this?

There are a number of reasons. First and foremost, flexibility in your performances. While the Ableton instruments are topnotch, combining them lets you make performance environments that allow you to do things on stage or in the studio that not only sound cool, but also make you feel more in control. For example, if I was using a Simpler—the mini sample playback instrument of Ableton Live—right now, I would be limited to working with one individual recorded audio file. Sure, I can filter it, tweak it, distort it, and mangle it, but it's still just that audio file.

With a Rack and those chained zones I spoke of in the previous chapter, I can easily move through multiple zones (as we did with effects) and access multiple patches in one Rack that can carry me through a whole performance. Or, I could double multiple sampled audio files, giving me a much bigger sound than I originally would've had access to, with the smaller sample player. I can even layer samples, Ableton synthesizers, and so much more.

So, let's try building an Instrument Rack now.

1. Let's build this Rack in an existing track in the project we've been building together. A bass patch would be an easy one to start with, so let's use our existing MIDI Bass track. So that you have a bit of uniformity, double-click on the title bar, where it says MIDI Bass, so that the instrument you're using for this track appears at the bottom. When it appears, click on it and press the Delete button to delete this device. When the bass device you were using is gone, drag an Instrument Rack from the Browser, as shown in Figure 6.1.

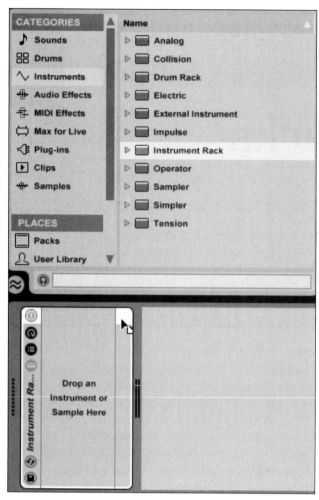

Figure 6.1 Add the Instrument Rack to a track.
Source: Ableton AG

2. Of course there is no sound if you try playing this track. The Instrument Rack in its default state is merely a container with nothing inside. Let's add some sound. First, add a Simpler to your brand-new Instrument Rack, as shown in Figure 6.2. As mentioned earlier in this chapter, Simpler is a very basic sample playback device, and by default there is no preloaded audio. You have to add some. I actually have some available for you at this address: www.cengageptr.com/downloads. When you have the samples for this patch, proceed to the next step.

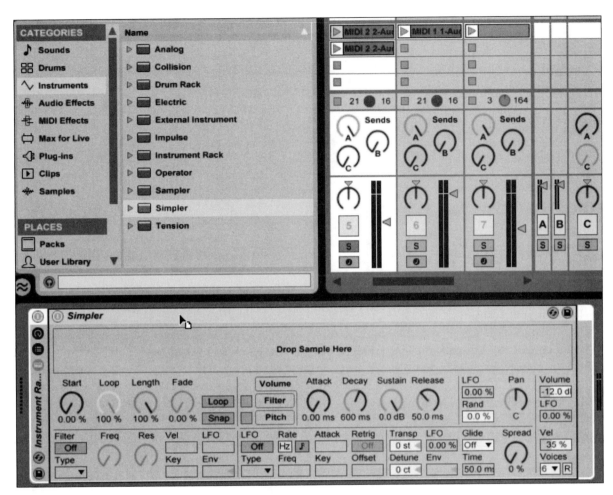

Figure 6.2 Add a Simpler to the Instrument Rack.
Source: Ableton AG

3. In the folder of sounds for this particular patch, you'll notice several audio files. If you've ever worked with a sampler before, you may think dialing in all of these files as separate samples will take a fair bit of time. It's true—setting up a multi-sample patch does tend to take some time. Not here, though. By simply dragging all of the audio files at once from an external browser window, you'll find that Live automatically sets up each audio file with its own Simpler and each Simpler within its own chain. Not bad, Ableton. Very slick, as a matter of fact. Try it yourself: Just drag each file into the "Drop an Instrument or Sample Here" section, as shown in Figure 6.3.

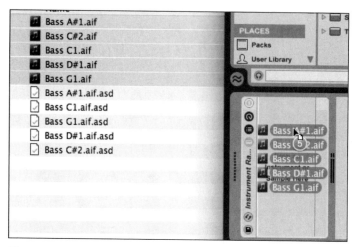

Figure 6.3 Drag files into an Instrument Rack from a Finder window.
Source: Ableton AG

4. Now that your Instrument Rack is populated with samples, add a touch of order. Trust me—this will really help when it's time to set up key zones. Order the chains so that they are listed in the order in which they would be played on a keyboard—for example, Bass C1, Bass D#1, and so on. See Figure 6.4 for reference. This isn't necessarily mandatory, mind you. It just keeps things simple later for programming and learning.

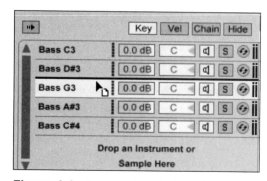

Figure 6.4 Reorder the chain order.
Source: Ableton AG

5. With the chains in order, you can begin zoning these Simplers within their respective chains so that your bass patch plays appropriately. Click the Key button at the top of the Chain List to access the Key Zone Editor, shown in Figure 6.5. As in most samplers and sample players, each audio file needs to be zoned and pitched so that it appropriately reproduces the synth patch you seek to emulate. You can do so easily with the Key Zone Editor.

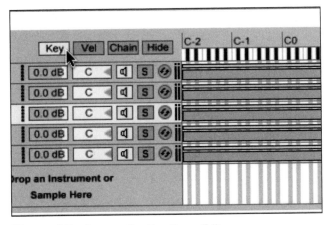

Figure 6.5 Access the Key Zone Editor.
Source: Ableton AG

6. In the Key Zone Editor, it's as simple as lining up which zone starts where. All you have to do is start Bass C3 at note C3 and cut it off before D#3. Then start Bass D#3 at D#3 and cut it off at G3. Repeat until finished. See Figure 6.6.

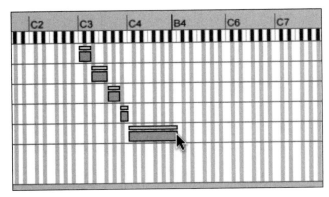

Figure 6.6 Zone key maps in the Key Zone Editor.
Source: Ableton AG

7. Now that everything is zoned, it's time to modify the starting note of each Simpler. To do this, use the Transpose function that is available on every Simpler in the Rack you are currently building. Unfortunately, Simpler does not have a root-note adjustment like most samplers. But I've taken care of the transposition values for you. C1 0, D#1 -3, G1 -7, A#1 -10, C#2 -13. Make these adjustments in each Simpler, as shown in Figure 6.7.

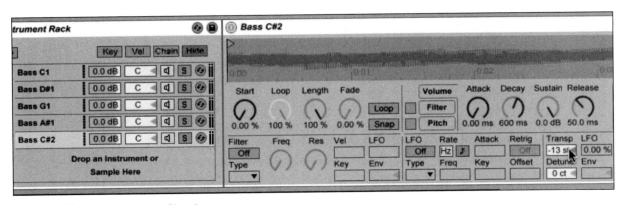

Figure 6.7 Transpose the Simpler.
Source: Ableton AG

8. For a moment, step back from the greater task of creating an Instrument Rack and focus on a basic setting in Simpler. Currently, you have several audio files being hosted by several Simplers. But you've probably noticed that if you sustain a key, the bass you're building eventually cuts out. This is because the synth audio files are not being looped. Now would be a good time to do this, before you venture further. Setting up audio to loop on Simpler is incredibly easy, and getting a decent, natural-sounding loop isn't too difficult. Enable Loop and Snap, as shown in Figure 6.8. Loop keeps the audio going as long as a key is held. Snap will help you locate a suitable loop point for each Simpler. Do this for each Simpler in the Rack. I suggest copying the Loop and Fade settings shown in Figure 6.8 as well. The Loop setting is just to tell Simpler what point to loop from within the audio file. Fade is a very cool setting that crossfades the Loop In and Loop Out points, so that you get a more natural-sounding loop point.

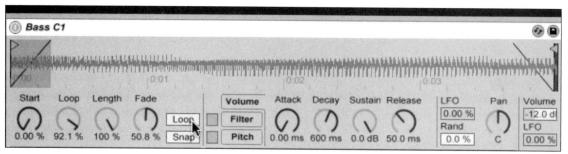

Figure 6.8 Enable Loop and Snap on Simpler.
Source: Ableton AG

9. You should have a much smoother and more polished-sounding Instrument Rack now. However, it's going to get much better. Now that the foundational stuff is out of the way, giving you a good, solid sound, you can start making the Instrument Rack work like a synthesizer. The best way to do this is to set up some macros. Synthesizers always have control over a filter. This is so easy to set up in an Instrument Rack! First, enable the Filter section for each Simpler, as shown in Figure 6.9. By default, each Simpler filter is set to Low-Pass 12. So, you'll be set up with a nice low-pass filter for your bass synth Instrument Rack.

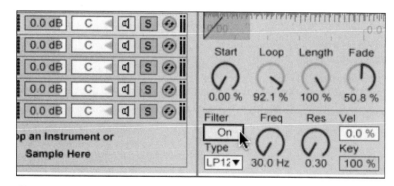

Figure 6.9 Enable the Simpler Filter.
Source: Ableton AG

10. Let's do the macros now. Assign each Freq (frequency) knob on each Simpler in the Rack to Macro 1. This will give your blooming instrument a Cutoff knob, essential for doing filter sweeps. Label Macro 1 *Cutoff* when you finish. When each Freq knob of each Simpler has been mapped to Macro 1 (now labeled Cutoff), map the Res (resonance) knob of each Simpler to Macro 2. Re-label this macro as *Res* when you're finished. See Figure 6.10.

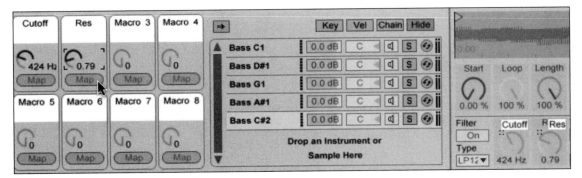

Figure 6.10 Set up and label macros.
Source: Ableton AG

11. Before you move on, play with the macro assignments you've made. Try boosting the Res, while lowering the Cutoff. You'll have even more fun with these features as you move forward.

12. You've got some control over the filters now, but it would be nice to have a little bit of polish. Bring in the filter envelope of the Simplers now, en masse, to add some punch to the bass. For this step, you'll need to enable a couple of things. The end result is very much worth it, though. First, you need to enable the actual filter envelope on each Simpler. This is just a simple toggle. Enable the filter envelope for each Simpler in each chain as shown in Figure 6.11.

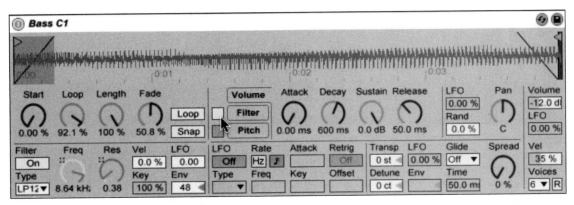

Figure 6.11 Enable the filter envelope.
Source: Ableton AG

13. With the filter envelope enabled, you need a way to give the envelope strength so that it effectively modulates the filter. Doing this shows another very interesting thing about what you can map and what you can't. Normally, you'd think that you can map only knobs. But you can, in fact, map to value displays as well. Your next mapping target will be the value display that determines the strength of the filter envelope. With the Map button pressed on the Instrument Rack, click the Env box in the Filter section of Simpler, shown in Figure 6.12. When that is clicked, press the Map button of Macro 3 to assign the Macro knob to this parameter. Map the Env (envelope value) box of each Simpler to Macro 3. Label the Macro as *Flt Env*. Once it's assigned, try playing with the setting with the filter cutoff (Macro 1) lowered. You can get a very percussive bass setting.

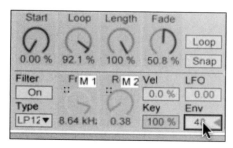

Figure 6.12 Assign envelope modulation to the filter of Simpler.
Source: Ableton AG

14. Now that the filter envelope has some strength and is actually doing something, let's make it even more expressive. Currently, the filter envelope is opening the low-pass filter that we have assigned to our Simplers only slightly. If you had a way to control the filter envelope decay, your patch could get much more expressive. This particular value isn't immediately available on a Simpler. As shown in Figure 6.13, you have to click the Filter page of the Envelope section to be able to access the filter envelope decay. Click the Filter page of the Envelope section now. Then, map the decay of the Filter Envelope section (of each Simpler) to Macro 4. Label this macro *Filter Decay*. This mapping allows you to make the filter envelope open up the filter much wider with keystrokes. It's also a great way to sculpt new basses on the fly.

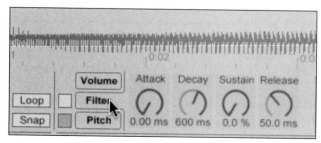

Figure 6.13 Simpler's filter envelope.
Source: Ableton AG

15. This bass is shaping up to be quite nice! But there's plenty more you could do with it. One option that may make things even more interesting would be to take advantage of Simpler's LFO capabilities. After all, LFO modulation is quite popular in modern dance music. Let's bring in a little "wobble," shall we? As with the filter envelope of Simpler, you'll need to give power to the LFO before it can become effective. But unlike the filter envelope, you may want to have the ability to completely disable the LFO if need be. So, map Macro 5 of each Simpler to the LFO Enable button, as shown in Figure 6.14. This gives you a means of completely disabling the LFO with a flip of the switch. In my opinion, this is a nice option because LFOs greatly change a bass's character. Label this macro *Wobble*.

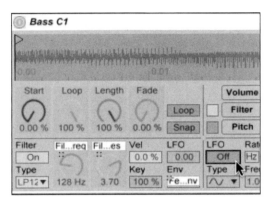

Figure 6.14 Map Macro 5 to the LFO Enable button.
Source: Ableton AG

16. Of course, you could rely on the LFO amount to disable and enable the LFO modulation, but by having a toggle and an incremental amount, you're setting yourself up for some nice abilities. For example, you can enable wobbles instantly in some cases and gradually add them in other cases. Let's add the ability to gradually add some wobble now. Map the filter LFO value box of each Simpler (shown in Figure 6.15) to Macro 6. Doing this will give you the ability to manually fade in modulation. Re-label Macro 6 as *Wobble Fade*.

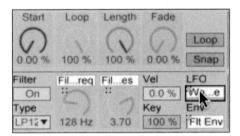

Figure 6.15 Map the filter LFO value box to Macro 6.
Source: Ableton AG

17. Of course, no wobbling bass-synth is complete without the ability to modify the rate of the wobble itself—the rate being the defining parameter that determines how fast the LFO modulates. On most samplers and synths, this parameter is named Rate. However, with Simpler, Ableton took a more true, scientific approach and went with Frequency—or Freq—which is found in the LFO section of Simpler, as shown in Figure 6.16. Map the Freq value box to Macro 7. Also, rename the macro to be *Wobble Rate*. By doing this, you can now make rapid frequency shifts. But don't take my word for it; try it with the filter Freq knob down quite low.

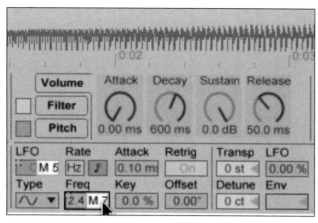

Figure 6.16 Map to the LFO frequency.
Source: Ableton AG

18. Finally, for the basic bass, take a stab at doing something very simple to give yourself a bigger sound. Simpler has one nice little parameter that spreads a mono recording over a stereo field. This parameter is known as Spread. Let's map the Spread, shown in Figure 6.17, of each Simpler to Macro 8. This will give you the quick ability to make your bass seem bigger on the fly. Note: This will thin the bass slightly in the bottom end but will almost give you the ability to use the bass as a lead. Experiment! Label this macro as *Fattener* when you're finished with all the mapping.

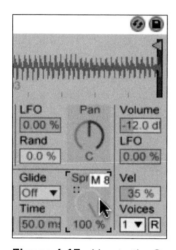

Figure 6.17 Map to the Spread parameter.
Source: Ableton AG

19. As a final nice touch, add a little color to your work…literally. You can actually change the hue and color of each macro. Try this: Right-click on a macro. At the bottom of the contextual menu that pops up, you'll notice several color blocks to choose from, as shown in Figure 6.18. Add some different colors of your choice to each of the macros you set up. This may sound a little trivial, but color is a great way to visually remember a function, and memory is more than helpful during live or studio performances. But another even handier reason to use color is that the colors you choose for each macro will also appear in the Mapping Browser. Later, when you've set up several different mappings and you want to modify increments of what does what, you'll find this extremely valuable when moving through the list.

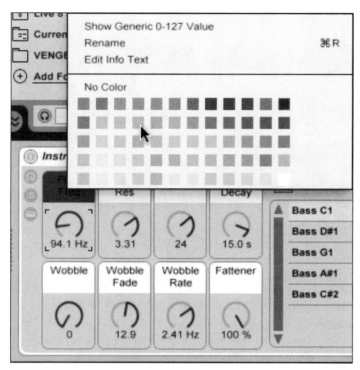

Figure 6.18 Change the colors of macros.
Source: Ableton AG

20. It might appear as if you're finished with your bass. And it's true—you could leave things as is. But you haven't even taken a look at effects within an Instrument Rack yet. This would be a wonderful way of adding some drive, some power, and some coolness to what you're doing. And, it will demonstrate a few more points, like the main one I'm about to make: You can have Racks within Racks.

Let's begin this next section and add in some greater depth to your bass. But before moving forward, make sure you save your work. You don't want to lose the patch you've spent so much time on!

Effects and Order within Instrument Racks

With the current state of things in your Instrument Rack, it would be difficult to assign any effects to live within the Rack for a few reasons. The main reason is that you would have to assign an effect to each chain. This would be annoying and would drain a lot of CPU. Also, with the Rack bulking up the way it is, this would be a great time to create some order by labeling. Let's do all of this now!

1. Your first step to getting some topnotch effects into your Instrument Rack is using a very simple but powerful feature: grouping. Basically, you can group the chains you've already created to make your bass Instrument Rack. And when you do this, something really fascinating happens: Another Rack appears within the Rack that you're building. Try this out yourself. Click Bass C1 and then hold the Shift button down and click Bass C#2. This will select all of your chains. Next, use the Command/Ctrl+G to group your chains. You can also right-click and use the contextual menu, as shown in Figure 6.19.

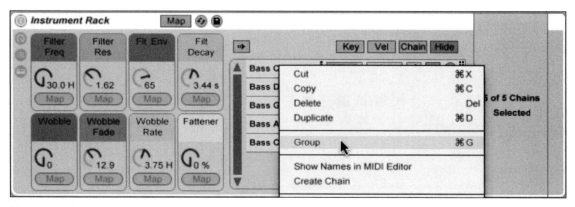

Figure 6.19 Group chains in the Instrument Rack.
Source: Ableton AG

2. Now that you've grouped your bass instrument as a chain unto itself, you have ample room to add in some effects. But before you move on, you should name the chain. In the newly created Chain List, you'll notice your Instrument Rack listed as yet another chain. Let's re-label this chain (Command/Ctrl+R) to *Basic Bass* (see Figure 6.20). This will help you differentiate any other instruments you might build in the future.

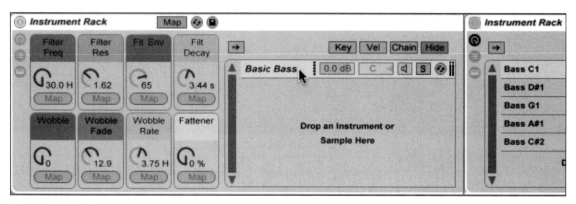

Figure 6.20 Rename the chain.
Source: Ableton AG

3. It's also important to note that you can rename the basic bass component or Rack that you built that is now living within your bigger Rack. It's actually helpful to rename the smaller Rack, as it can help differentiate each component within the Rack as it builds up. Click on the title bar of the bass Instrument Rack within your Instrument Rack and use Command/Ctrl+R to rename the device, as shown in Figure 6.21. It may seem silly to do all of this labeling, but Racks can get very big and confusing. The more you label, the easier it is to retrace your steps. It is programming, after all. Think of this as a form of debugging.

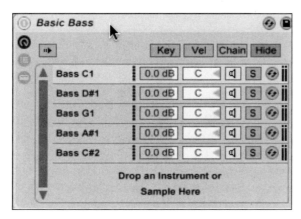

Figure 6.21 Rename a Rack within a Rack.
Source: Ableton AG

4. To create space and because you know that you'll be adding some more stuff to your Rack, fold down what you've built. To do this, double-click on the title bar of your Basic Bass Rack within your Rack. This will cause the internal Rack to fold down, giving you much more room to work and see. This means less scrolling around. See Figure 6.22.

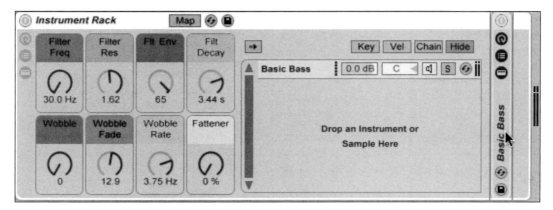

Figure 6.22 Fold down components within the Rack.
Source: Ableton AG

5. All right, now that everything is tidied up, you can easily drop in some effects. For your first effect, drop in a chorus. To do this, drop the chorus on the Basic Bass chain, in the now encapsulating Instrument Rack, over your other Instrument Rack. This will cause the chorus to appear within the current Rack's brackets, as shown in Figure 6.23. If you play a note or two, you'll notice that the chorus is now affecting all chains in the bass Instrument Rack.

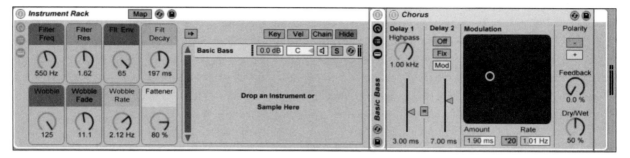

Figure 6.23 Add a chorus to a chain in the Instrument Rack.
Source: Ableton AG

6. With the addition of the chorus in your Instrument Rack, you're free to have a little more fun. Remember, you can map macros to multiple functions and multiple devices within a Rack. Let's take advantage of this feature now. One trick for disabling and enabling the chorus is to assign it to a macro that goes along with the whole fattening thing that a chorus adds to the mix. Why don't we map the chorus to the fattener macro? To do this, you can map the Dry/Wet knob of the chorus to the Fattener macro knob. Do this now. Also, rename the chorus by re-labeling its title bar to *Fattener*. See Figure 6.24. You might as well continue keeping order in your system, right?

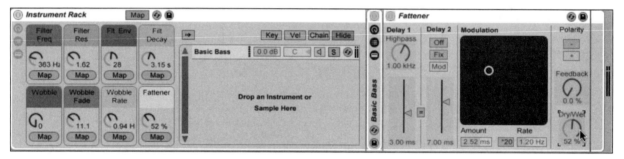

Figure 6.24 Map the Dry/Wet knob on a re-labeled chorus.
Source: Ableton AG

7. You can also have a little fun by making the chorus (fattener) more modulation-happy. Two other parameters you can integrate into the macro system you've devised are the rate and the amount of the chorus (fattener) itself. Let's assign these functions to the wobble rate and amount. This way you keep some consistency, right? Map the amount of the chorus to the Wobble Fade macro. Map the rate of the chorus to the Wobble Rate macro. See Figure 6.25. What will happen when you do this? The rapid modulation added to the wobble will make this bass full of intense modulation. But, even better, when the wobble is off, you can still add some nice modulation and control it with the Wobble Fade and Rate knobs.

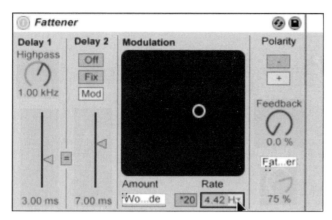

Figure 6.25 Map the chorus amount and rate.
Source: Ableton AG

8. You can also add multiple additional effects, if you'd like. Personally, I wouldn't mind a reverb to make things a little fuller and more vibrant. Drop a Reverb device from the Ableton Browser onto the Basic Bass chain within the instrument Browser. If you'd like, you can double-click on the title bar of the Fattener (chorus) to make some more room for editing the reverb as well, as shown in Figure 6.26.

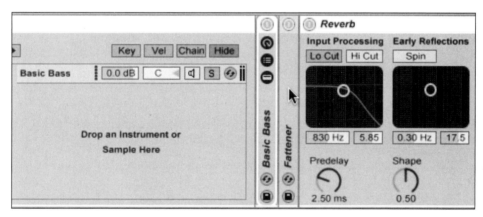

Figure 6.26 Drop a reverb in a chain, alongside a condensed chorus.
Source: Ableton AG

9. For this particular effect, you don't necessarily need to worry about assigning anything as a macro. Getting some nice settings in there to complete your bass atmosphere is good enough. I suggest keeping the quality of the reverb set at Eco, for economical. This keeps the reverb from straining your processor too much. Also, I'd keep the decay time relatively low, around 1.02s. This is a bass patch, after all. And you don't want to muddy things up too much by having a long trail behind every note played. Finally, I suggest playing with the Dry/Wet knob and getting it set to your preference. See Figure 6.27 for my settings.

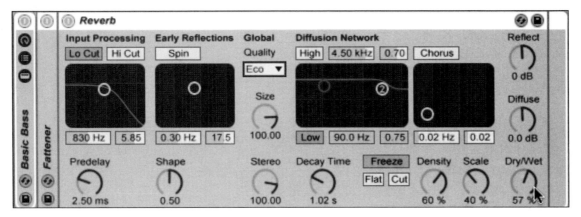

Figure 6.27 Reverb settings.

Source: Ableton AG

10. Finally, it would be good to save your hard work. Not as a song or project, per se, but as an Instrument Rack that can be accessed again for any song. To do this, click the small Save button at the top of the Instrument Rack. This will cause a section of the Browser to highlight a section of the user library. Name your Rack *Big Bass* or whatever suits your fancy. When you want to access this in the future, simply refer to this area of the User Library.

Well, you've made your first Live instrument! And while there were a few steps, I'd like to think that it was a lot of fun. In the next chapter, we'll move on to creating a Drum Rack. Make sure you're all saved up.

Drum Racks

IN THE PREVIOUS CHAPTER, you got a great overview of making incredible instruments with Instrument Racks in Ableton Live. In this chapter, we'll continue with the theme of instrument creation, but this time you'll create percussive instruments instead—namely, drums.

The Drum Rack, another container-style device within Ableton Live, is remarkably engineered for not only quick, but also thorough drum-patch creation and modification. Its mix section is dramatically enhanced and caters to percussion. For example, the Drum Rack has sends and returns of its own and can host multiple inserts per drum... and it can hold a lot of drums.

For this Drum Rack, I've included samples that you can download here: www.cengageptr.com/downloads. This is just a basic kit. However, you'll be doing some advanced stuff to make these rather mediocre drum sounds even better.

All right, let's get started!

1. Create a new MIDI track in Ableton Live and drag Drum Rack from the Instruments view of the Browser onto the new track (see Figure 7.1). If you'd like, you can also simply add an empty Drum Rack onto the existing drum track you've been using throughout this book. But I'll warn you, all the drum parts may not transfer over exactly. You can also create a new drum beat to throw into the song you've been building, using the Drum Rack you're about to make.

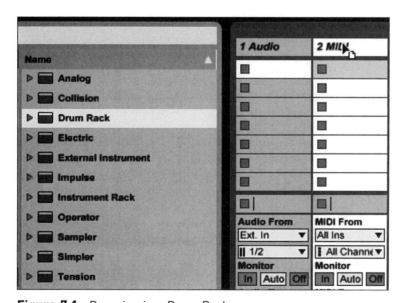

Figure 7.1 Dragging in a Drum Rack.
Source: Ableton AG

2. You'll notice that the Rack that appears is very different from what you've seen before. The grid labeled with different notes is reminiscent of the classic drum machine button grid, so prominent on the Akai MPC series of drum machines and so on. And while it appears that there are only 16 assignable buttons on this grid, don't be fooled. If you scroll along the Pad Overview on the left, shown in Figure 7.2, you'll discover that there are several pads that can be assigned samples. Try clicking and scrolling along this Pad Overview now. If you're using a laptop's trackpad, like on a MacBook Pro, note that you can use a two-finger scroll up and down to move through the different pads.

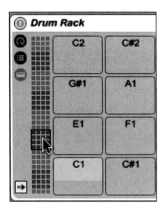

Figure 7.2 The Pad Overview in the Drum Rack.
Source: Ableton AG

3. Now that you have some level of familiarity with the Drum Rack pads, let's assign a sample to a pad. Locate the Drum Rack folder in the sound file you downloaded. In this folder, drag Kick 1 to the pad labeled C1, within the Drum Rack pads. You'll notice that as soon as you do this, the pad will become much more complex, as new, smaller buttons are added to it (see Figure 7.3). These smaller buttons are the M (Mute) and S (Solo) buttons and a preview button, which looks like an arrow pointing to the right. If you hover over the pad, a small Hot Swap button will appear, allowing you to swap out sounds from your Live Library as well. Try locating the C1 key on your MIDI controller or QWERTY keyboard and triggering the kick drum, C1.

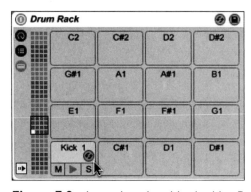

Figure 7.3 An assigned pad in the Live Drum Rack.
Source: Ableton AG

> **IMPORTING SOUNDS:** You can drag a sample from a Finder or Explorer window into the Drum Rack. You do not have to do this from Ableton Live's Browser. Dragging samples from within the Browser works exactly the same way as dragging in a sound from another location on the computer. Also, it's important to know that regular WAV and AIF files are the preferred audio file types for the Drum Rack, Simpler, Sampler, and other audio playback devices within Ableton Live.

4. Before moving on to the other drum sounds, let's get the kick drum nice and beefed up. We all learned to start from the kick when building up a mix, so let's do the same when building a Rack. Of course, you know you need a compressor for a kick drum. So, drag a compressor from the Audio Effects category of the Browser onto the kick pad in the Drum Rack. Once the compressor is in, you'll need to condense some stuff (such as the Simpler hosting the kick sample) by double-clicking on the title bar so that it's minimized. Or, just scroll over to the compressor. Once you reach the compressor, click the Show Activity View button, shown in Figure 7.4. This gives you a much more comprehensive way to view your compression input and output.

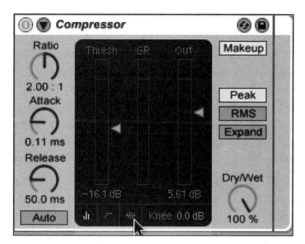

Figure 7.4 Press the Show Activity View button on the compressor.
Source: Ableton AG

5. Now, let's really set up the compressor and make this "kick." Lower the Knee to 0, so that you can get some hard compression. In higher settings, Knee is nice for vocals, guitar, more dynamic drums (jazz), and so on because it causes the compression to kick in gradually as the threshold level is approached. Because we're working on a dance electronica kit, we want precision. So, the compression needs to kick in as soon as the threshold level is passed. To set up the threshold, move the dark orange line in the middle of the Compressor screen down until it sits just past the peak of the kick drum when played. It should be around –14.2 dB. See Figure 7.5. This will give your bass a little more bite and will bring out some of that low end.

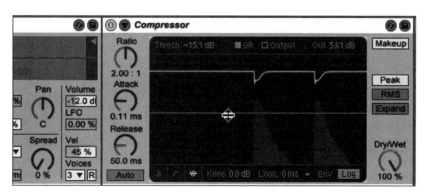

Figure 7.5 Adjust the threshold on the compressor.
Source: Ableton AG

SIMPLER AND DRUM RACKS: Like the Instrument Rack, the Drum Rack automatically manufactures Simplers for every sound you bring into your Drum Rack. This allows you to assemble Drum Racks very quickly and eliminates the need to figure out what sound will be what. But don't think that you're limited to working only with Simplers. You can use synths such as Analog, Sampler, Operator, and so on as well. Because these instruments aren't included with every version of Live, I'm going with the basic instruments so that there's no chance you don't have it!

6. To complete your Compressor settings, boost the Output to 5.61 dB. At this level, the kick is more than audible and will stand up to whatever you put near it. Let's also lower the Attack to .11 ms. This gives you a very quick bit of compression on the beginning of the kick (squashing the click), and then with the boosted output, you get a much bigger tail of nice low end. Now, you should have one mighty kick drum to build around. See Figure 7.6.

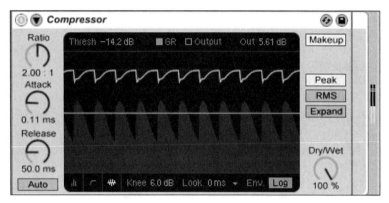

Figure 7.6 Final compression settings.
Source: Ableton AG

PREFERENCE: Feel free to play with the compression settings. After all, we all have different tastes. You may also wish to try some different views on the Compressor for dialing things in. Try the Show Transfer Curve view or the Collapsed view. Whatever helps you get your sound...

7. Before moving on to another drum, you may also want to apply some EQ. Because your kick is very thick, it might be nice to shave off a little bit of the low end. Again, this is pure preference, but it's important to at least know that you have the option in the Drum Rack. Drag an EQ Eight onto the kick drum pad. Once the EQ Eight is loaded and active, enable the Filter 1 activator. With Filter 1 now selected, set the frequency to 52 Hz, as shown in Figure 7.7. By doing this, you are cutting some of the more powerful low-end frequencies your monitors may not allow you to hear. You'll notice that as you play the kick drum, lots of low-end frequencies are jumping up in the frequency display of EQ Eight. This small bit of cutting just helps you keep the beast of a kick drum under control. By adding this EQ Eight, it demonstrates again that you can easily keep adding inserts to all of your channels. You aren't limited. But for sanity's sake, you may want to go with what you need, if you know what I mean.

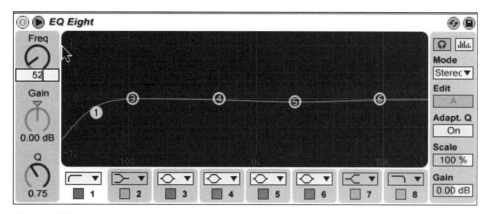

Figure 7.7 Adjusting the Freq on the EQ Eight.
Source: Ableton AG

8. All right, one more thing before we move to another drum. Let's set up a return in the Drum Rack, so that you can build an environment and not blow up your processor. To the left of the Drum Pad Overview, you'll notice an S and an R button. Click the R button. This will cause a small Drop Audio Effects Here box to appear below the Chain List. Drop a reverb onto this box, as shown in Figure 7.8. We'll come back to the reverb settings later. For now, you have it available for all of your drums, and you don't have to worry about four or five hidden reverbs that you don't actually need building up.

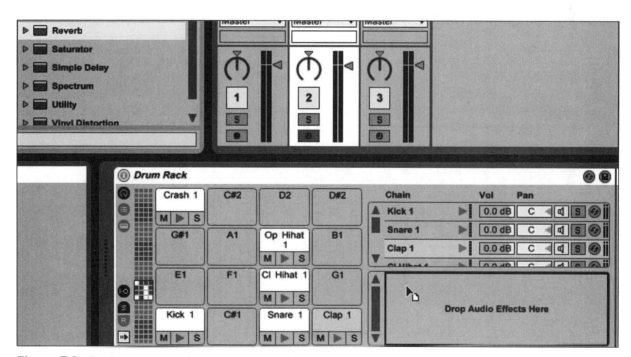

Figure 7.8 Setting up a reverb as a return in the Drum Rack.
Source: Ableton AG

9. Now let's add in another drum. There's no better drum to add next than the snare drum. Drag Snare 1.wav onto the D1 Drum Rack pad and try triggering the sound. I suggest adding the snare to your MIDI drum beat, maybe on Beats 2 and 4.

Going Pro with Ableton Live

10. As you can hear, it's not really that interesting of a snare drum. Let's tweak it a little bit. I found that raising its pitch a semitone brightened it up just a bit (see Figure 7.9). Give this a try, or even try modifying the pitches up or down if you'd like. I also encourage you to make a drum beat MIDI loop at this point. Use the Session View and just make a beat with the snare and kick. This will really help dial in the sound of your kit as you move along.

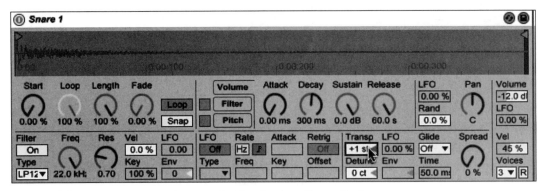

Figure 7.9 Pitch the snare drum up in Simpler in a Drum Rack.

Source: Ableton AG

11. With the snare drum dialed in, in terms of pitch, let's get some reverb on it. Click the S button next to the R (Return) button on the left of the Drum Rack pad, as shown in Figure 7.10. This expands the available parameters within the Chain List, beyond Level, Pan, Solo, and so on. And, it gives you access to the sends for each chain. So, to give the snare a little reverb, increase the send amount on the Chain List for Snare 1. Just click and hold in the value box in the Send A column and drag up. You can also click in the box and then type the value in dB that you'd like. My value is set to −5.3. You may notice that even at high settings, the reverb signal seems a little weak. Don't worry; we still need to tweak the reverb.

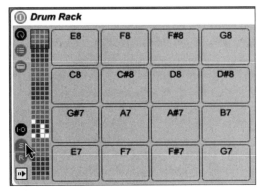

Figure 7.10 Press a button to show sends.

Source: Ableton AG

12. Click on the reverb chain in the Chain List and scroll over to the Reverb module itself. At this moment, the reverb is in its default state. Choose a preset with the Hot Swap feature that will do the trick for not just your snare, but also a few other channels. To initiate the Hot Swap command, press the Q button while the reverb is selected in the Drum Rack. Check out the Warm Reverb Long in the Hall subcategory, as shown in Figure 7.11. I chose this one because I could easily see this effect being used for multiple sounds as the Drum Rack continues to build. As you demo your own reverb settings, keep in mind that the reverb presets tend to

have the Dry/Wet setting at about 55%. For insert effects, this is a good default setting. But because you're using the reverb as a return effect, you'll want to crank each Dry/Wet knob to 100%.

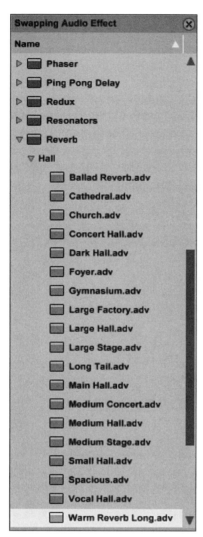

Figure 7.11 Hot-swap reverb presets in the Browser.
Source: Ableton AG

13. Okay, you've got a nice reverb for one return effect, and this will carry you for a while. Let's add another sound to your Drum Rack. This time, select Clap 1.wav from the Drum Rack folder. Drag this audio file onto D#1. For this particular audio file/sample, you'll need to do a little bit more work with Simpler to get it to "pop." One easy way to get the clap to stand out nicely is by using Simpler's built-in filter. Enable Clap 1 Simpler's filter and switch it to BP12 (Band Pass). Now, edge the Freq knob over to 1.45 kHz. This will automatically cut off some of the low and high end from the clap sound. And this is fine—it needs to be a little midrange. This will help it sit nicely! You can also push these mid- to high-range frequencies with the Res (Resonance) knob. It ends up giving the clap that kind of "popping" sound. Move the Res knob up to 0.82, as shown in Figure 7.12, or experiment even more. It would also be helpful to add a little reverb to the clap. Raise the send level to –14.0. This will give the clap that nice tail that fades out a little slower.

Figure 7.12 Modify Simpler's filter settings.

Source: Ableton AG

14. Let's start working on the hi-hat now—which is, of course, two samples. Starting with Cl Hihat 1 (closed hi-hat), place this audio file on F#1. For Op Hihat 1 (open hi-hat), place this audio file on A#1. See Figure 7.13 for a reference of what the Drum Rack pads look like currently. Also, add some hi-hats to your drum beat at this point. They aren't dialed in, of course. But this will help you do it. Set up some hi-hat MIDI activity in your drum beat, too. Remember, in Session mode, if you start recording on a clip that already has MIDI data, you can simply overdub. Try to do a 16 beat if you can. This will be a lot of fun for what's coming up: sidechain.

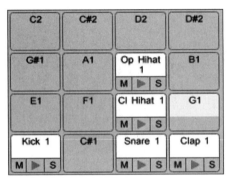

Figure 7.13 The drum pad arrangement at this point.

Source: Ableton AG

GENERAL MIDI: The key arrangement that I've chosen for this patch is purposeful. The General MIDI style of mapping is a common mapping toward which many sound designers tend to gravitate. It generally consists of C1 on kick, C1 for snare, clap on D#1, and so on. You might continue to use this mapping as you move forward so that you can keep some uniformity in your kits.

15. With the hi-hats mapped, it's time to make some modifications. First investigate the open hi-hat. You can use the filter to shelve off any unneeded frequencies—in this case, the low frequencies that no cymbal ever uses. After enabling the filter on both Simplers for the closed and open hi-hat, set the Filter Type to HP12 (High Pass) and the Freq to 1.06 kHz for both, as shown in Figure 7.14. As a suggestion, you may also want to remove the key tracking for the filter. This setting causes the filter to open and close based on the keys pressed. Because only one key can be pressed, it's a non-issue. But it doesn't hurt to remove it for a chance of some additional coloration.

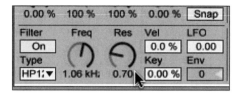

Figure 7.14 Set the Filter Type to HP12 and the Freq to 1.06 kHz.
Source: Ableton AG

> **MY PATTERN:** In case you're interested, I'm using a very simple pattern for this exercise—just a basic 16 beat with the kick hitting on 1, 1.2, 1.3, and 1.4 and the snare hitting on 1.2 and 1.4. As we get into the sidechain effect, you may want to set up a MIDI pattern like this for your Drum Rack, if only for the purposes of demonstration.

16. Now, here's where you can have a little additional fun with the hi-hats. Let's take a look at setting up a sidechain scenario within the Drum Rack. If you remember, in the previous chapter you were able to group part of your Instrument Rack's chains within itself. This created an additional Instrument Rack within the Instrument Rack. Grouping chains is available within the Drum Rack as well. But with the Drum Rack, this gives you an added perk, because you usually want to be able to submix parts of drum kits. Select the Cl Hihat 1 chain and then Shift-select the Op Hihat 1 chain. Now use the Command/Ctrl+G shortcut to group these two chains. As with the Instrument Rack grouping you did, another Drum Rack is created in your Drum Rack. Click on the Drum Rack label and use Command/Ctrl+R to re-label this internal Rack to *Hihats* (see Figure 7.15).

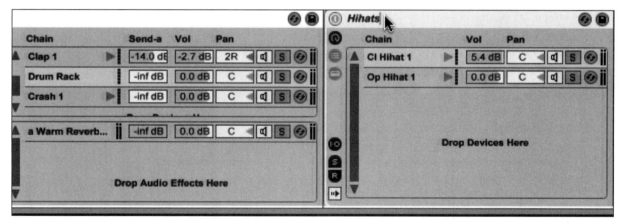

Figure 7.15 Re-label a sub–Drum Rack.
Source: Ableton AG

17. With both hi-hat components grouped, you can now assign an insert that will affect both cymbals only. This can be useful for several reasons, but in this case, I just want a compressor on both samplers so that we can sidechain them. Drag a compressor onto the newly created Hihats chain. Once the compressor is applied, click the Sidechain toggle button in the upper-left corner of the Compressor interface, as shown in Figure 7.16.

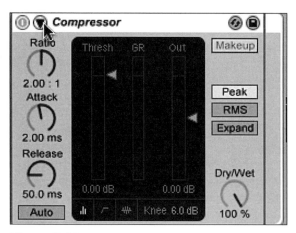

Figure 7.16 Click the Sidechain toggle button.
Source: Ableton AG

18. To be honest, I am a huge fan of the dedicated sidechain panels on the compressor, the gate, and several of the other Live effects. Unlike in some of the other DAWs, these subpanels make sidechaining extremely easy to set up. For example, in Logic you have to set up a bus, send to the bus…it's a long process. Let's try this out now. In the Sidechain section of your Hihat channel compressor, enable Sidechain. Then choose the Drum Rack, as it's currently labeled as your Audio From source. When you choose this, a submenu will appear. Choose Drum Rack Kick 1 Pre FX as the specific source. See Figure 7.17. By doing this, you're setting up the kick drum to modulate the compressor with a clean signal, as opposed to post FX processing.

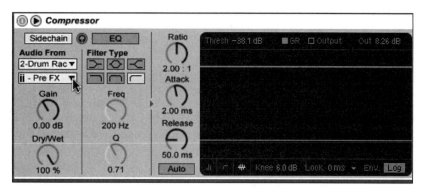

Figure 7.17 Setting up the Sidechain section of the compressor.
Source: Ableton AG

19. All right, with the sidechain now active, let's make some adjustments to the Compressor section. Keep in mind, the settings we're making are more for the sidechain "pumping effect" than the regular old compression settings. If you're looking for natural-sounding settings, it's best to apply the settings in this step and then adjust until they sound right to your ears. First, switch the Compressor view to Show Activity view. This will actually allow you to see what you're doing, and you can make modifications as you see fit. Once in this view, lower the orange line (Threshold) until it's comfortably past the peaks of the hi-hat spikes, as shown in Figure 7.18. You're really trying to squash the signal so that you can hear the sidechain effect in action. Now raise the Compression Ratio setting to 5:00:1, so that your compression is again much more severe. This will also augment the pumping effect to be applied to the hi-hats by squashing much more. But, it will also lower the perceived volume because of so much squash. Therefore, let's raise the Output Level to 15.2. Now, you can hear things again, but it probably sounds much different.

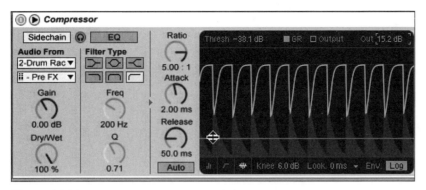

Figure 7.18 Adjust the threshold in Sidechain mode.
Source: Ableton AG

KICK AND SIDECHAIN: Now, because the kick has a long decay, it might be good to pull back on the tail a little bit with the Kick 1 sampler's own amplitude envelope. The reason why the tail of the kick is an issue is that the kick is the modulating source of the hi-hats now. Quicker hi-hat bursts will be hard because if you're running more than a couple of kick hits within your pattern, the hi-may be completely reduced. But because the kick is so long, it won't hurt anything to make it just a little shorter. Access the Kick 1 Simpler in the Drum Rack chain and reduce the Decay until the sidechaining sounds more open.

Keep in mind that the effect will sound different depending on the beat you're using. As I mentioned in an earlier tip, I'm using a standard club, 16 beat, and this effect was designed around this kind of beat. But it's equally cool for hip-hop and other genres; you just have to use it a little differently at times. Regardless, you're here to learn how to set this up in Ableton, with features specific to Ableton. Let's keep rolling!

20. Now that you can hear the effect, basically, in action, let's up the ante. Raise the Gain knob in the Sidechain section to about 10.7 dB. This increases the amount of kick modulation coming in and causes the compressor to push the hi-hats much more severely. This is also a fun time to adjust the Attack and Release. Take the Attack down to .10 ms. This will cause the initial hit of the hi-hat to be much more subdued. Now raise the Release, as shown in Figure 7.19, to 250 ms. Because the Release is causing the compression to stay on a little longer on each hit now, you actually start to get different perceived rhythmic patterns. Notice, in Figure 7.19, how much the output pattern has changed.

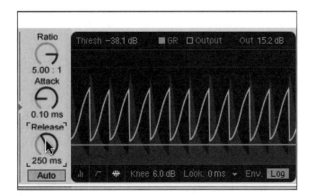

Figure 7.19 Modify the Release to modify a rhythmic pattern.
Source: Ableton AG

21. All right, with the hi-hats locked in, it's time to finish this kit by adding the crash. Drop Crash 1.wav onto C#2 and add a crash hit in your MIDI pattern. See Figure 7.20. Just one hit at the beginning of your MIDI drum beat will be fine. For this particular crash, there's not a lot of work that needs to be done. Really, apply some reverb on the send that you set up, and you're basically done. Let's move on to mixing now.

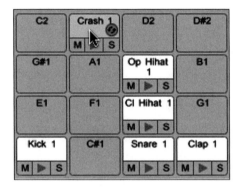

Figure 7.20 Add the crash to the Drum Rack pads.
Source: Ableton AG

22. Here's where things get even more fun! Now it's time to mix what you've set up in this Drum Rack. Click on the small arrow next to the title bar, where it says Drum Rack, shown in Figure 7.21. This opens up the Drum Rack like a group in the Session View. From here, you can mix the drums in a way that sounds good and appropriate. And, all the settings you make within these grouped channels will be reflected in the Chain List of the Drum Rack as well. However, you'll note that the sends and pan knobs, as well as the MIDI From, Monitor, and all that other stuff, look very different on these channels. In these channels that are specific to the Drum Rack, let's begin moving some things around in Volume and Pan. The Pan boxes currently show a value of C, for Center. Click hold and drag to the right the Snare channel, so that 2L is listed. This just puts the snare off slightly to the left. For the Clap, place it over to 2R. It will be slightly to the right, and this will give it a space in the stereo field. For the hi-hats, mix those guys over a little farther to the left with an 11L setting. This will help emulate the setup of drum placement onstage. You know how the hi-hats are usually a little left or right of the snare drum? I always go with left. It's your preference, though—especially if you're trying to emulate your favorite drummer. Finally, let's put the Crash over at 11R, where the crash usually is within a drum set...or some drum sets.

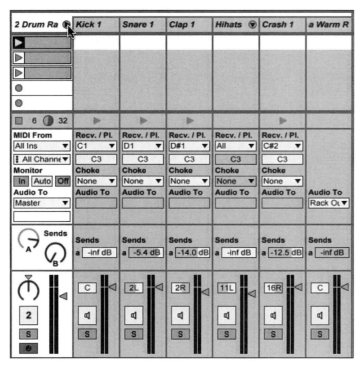

Figure 7.21 Mix the Drum Rack.
Source: Ableton AG

23. Last but not least, save your Drum Rack. Click the Save Preset button on the Drum Rack device, shown in Figure 7.22. In the Browser, the title will still list Drum Rack in orange. Type in the name for your Drum Rack. I'm just going to call mine *Electronic Kit*, as this is a very accurate description. You can name it whatever you like.

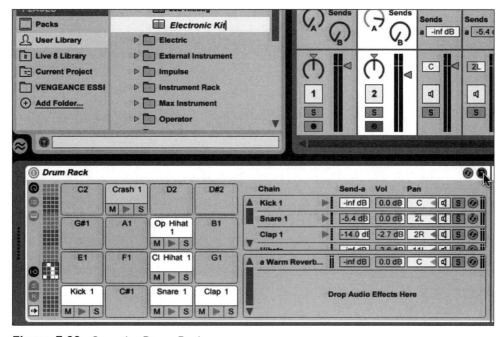

Figure 7.22 Save the Drum Rack.
Source: Ableton AG

All right, this wraps up our foray through the wide world of Drum Rack creation. Remember, you can add all sorts of devices into Drum Racks besides the devices we used in this chapter. Try to experiment with not only samples, but with instruments, too.

Also, remember that you can also use third-party plug-ins in Racks. Don't feel as if you have to go with the Ableton devices. I haven't shown third-party plug-ins because I want to make sure you have everything you need to complete these exercises.

In the next tutorial, we'll look at some final pieces of polish in Ableton Live before we wrap things up. See you there!

Specific Needs

B Y THIS POINT, we've covered the major components of Ableton Live 9. But there are still specific features that you'll need, based on what you're using Live for professionally. In this chapter, I'll focus on helping you get to those specific tasks, such as DJing, scoring, and so on.

For this final chapter, save your current project but keep it handy—you'll need it later in this chapter. For the moment, let's start by talking about DJing!

DJ Setup

Live is actually a formidable DJ platform for a number of reasons. Personally, I think audio warping is its main asset. ...uld be equally easy to say that the Session View is another major reason unto itself. The grid-style ability ....ger tracks, the crossfader... Oh, I think it's time we talked about the crossfader. Let's go ahead and begin now.

1. In a new Ableton project, set up two audio tracks. Because these two tracks will be your Deck A and Deck B for your DJ set, label Track 1 as *A* and Track 2 as *B*, as shown in Figure 8.1. These two tracks will act as your turntables.

Figure 8.1 Begin setup for the DJ project.
Source: Ableton AG

2. With the two tracks set up, it's a good time to locate the file load of MP3s you'll be using for DJing. In many cases, this will be iTunes. If this is the case, simply drag the iTunes folder on your hard drive into the Places section of the Browser, as shown in Figure 8.2. You can then use these audio files from iTunes within Live. If you have your music in a different location on your drive, simply drag this file into the Browser. You can also click the Add Folder button at the bottom of the Places section. Keep in mind that you can also break down different folders, so that they appear individually in the Browser. Just drag each folder into the Ableton Browser individually if this serves you best.

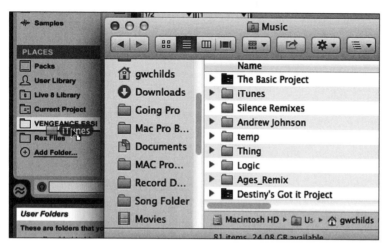

Figure 8.2 Add music locations to Ableton's Browser.
Source: Ableton AG

FILE TYPES: Ableton reads MP3 files but not AAC files. With that being said, before you head to a DJ gig you may want to examine which audio files in your library will work in Ableton and which won't.

---

3. When you've set up your Places to include all the locations of your audio files for DJing, click the Show/Hide Crossfader Section button. This button is located in the vicinity of the Show/Hide I-O section and the rest of the Show/Hide buttons you've been using throughout this book, as shown in Figure 8.3. When you click this button, it reveals sets of A/B buttons on each audio channel and a crossfader on the master channel of Ableton Live.

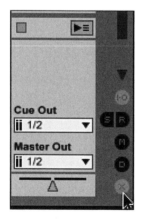

Figure 8.3 Click the Show/Hide Crossfader Section button.
Source: Ableton AG

4. Now that the Crossfader section is revealed, you'll note that you have access to the actual crossfader available in the master channel, shown in Figure 8.4. The idea is very simple—select A on the first audio channel you set up, which is your A deck. On the B channel, select B. Once the A and B tracks are selected, you can use the Master track crossfader to fade between the A and B audio tracks. Try crossfading on your own to get a feel for it. Simply cue an audio clip on each track and fade back and forth with the crossfader.

Figure 8.4 Crossfade with Ableton Live.
Source: Ableton AG

5. At this point, you probably have some concerns about monitoring your cued tracks so that you can beat-match and simply know where to crossfade into certain sections to and from certain points in pieces of music. This is also taken care of within the master channel, specifically in the I-O section. Shown in Figure 8.5, you can use the master channel I-O section to determine which output of your audio interface will be the cued channel and the master out. If you have an audio interface with multiple audio outputs, select the cued audio output channel and the master. If you're using only your laptop's, built-in audio device, select Mono Channel 1 for cued and Mono Channel 2 for master.

Figure 8.5 Set up cue and master outputs.
Source: Ableton AG

6. With the cued and master audio outputs set up, it's time to set up a way to cue audio on the second audio track so that you can monitor what's going on aside from the master output. Click the Solo/Cue toggle on the master channel so that it says Cue. With the Cue mode enabled, the Solo buttons now become monitoring buttons. In fact, you'll notice that each solo button now has a tiny headphone where the S used to be. When you're in Cue mode, when you click the individual headphone buttons on any of the audio tracks, the track will be heard through the cued audio. To get used to this system, try running both tracks at once, crossfading and cueing, by clicking the headphone buttons. See Figure 8.6.

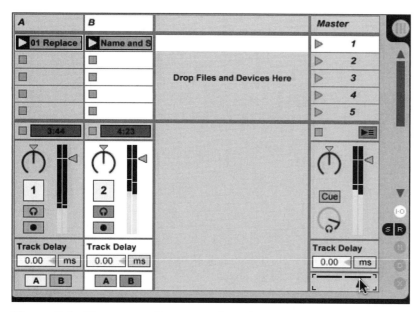

Figure 8.6 The cue monitor system in action.
Source: Ableton AG

7. Now that you have a few songs going in your DJ set, it's a good time to start looking through the Browser for new material. Make sure the Preview button (in the Browser) is clicked, as shown in Figure 8.7, and click on another song file within the Browser. This will cause the selected song to play in your cue monitor but not your master out. Once you decide you have a song you like, drag it into a clip slot.

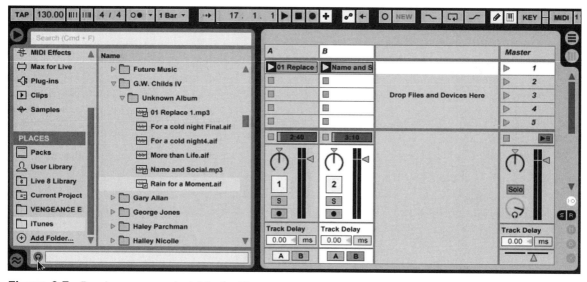

Figure 8.7 Preview song material in the Browser.
Source: Ableton AG

BROWSER LAG: The Browser sometimes takes a few seconds to load a song-file preview. This is usually because it's the Browser's first time playing the file. After a file has been played once, an Ableton analysis file will be placed in the directory where the audio file is. This means that the next time you play the audio file, it will preview much faster. To avoid the lag, go through a practice set and preview the audio files you know you want to use.

RAW VERSUS WARPED: When the Raw button is enabled in the Browser, as shown in Figure 8.8, audio retains its tempo regardless of what Ableton's host clock tempo is. When Raw is disabled, Preview mode in the Browser will play the song file warped at the tempo of your current set. Warped preview can cause the preview to take a bit longer, but if you're trying to beat-match the songs in your DJ set, keep Raw disabled so that the songs in the Browser are automatically warped to match your set. However, I should mention that relying on Auto Warp to warp all of your audio files accordingly could end in disastrous results. My best advice is to warp your own audio or at least double-check Auto Warp's work in advance.

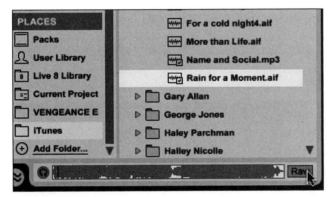

Figure 8.8 The Raw setting in the Browser Preview section.

Source: Ableton AG

Now that you have all of the elements you need for DJing, it might be time to add a little controller functionality for the crossfader, tempo, and so on. Let's take a look at this now.

Mapping Knobs to Controllers

Ableton Live allows you to have an unbelievable number of control mappings for external MIDI controllers. Continuing with the current DJ/song file, let's add some mappings into your MIDI controllers.

1. Click the MIDI button in the upper-right corner of Ableton Live. This toggles you into MIDI Map mode. When in this mode, you only need to move a knob, button, or fader on your MIDI controller, and you'll automatically see Ableton register a small label next to the chosen map assignment, as shown in Figure 8.9.

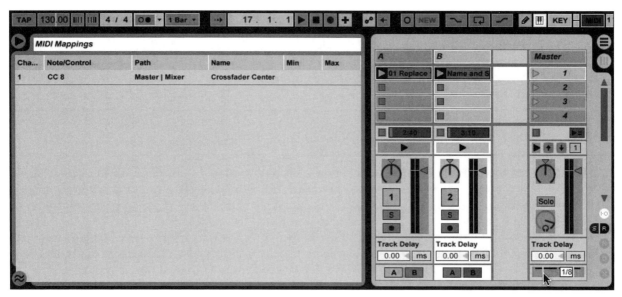

Figure 8.9 Map a controller to the Ableton crossfader.
Source: Ableton AG

2. Aside from Ableton registering your assignment near the physical location of the mapping assignment, you'll also see a map assignment in the Mapping Browser. Try doing what's described here. After you click the MIDI button at the top of Ableton, click on the crossfader with your mouse cursor, and then move a knob or fader on your controller that you'd like to assign to the crossfader.

3. Toggle off the MIDI Mapping mode by clicking the MIDI button in the upper-right corner of the Ableton interface again. Now, let's get some effects in that are directly necessary for DJing. Add some EQ. Drag an EQ Eight onto Track A and Track B. In EQ Eight, change the Filter mode on Filter 3 to Low Cut. On Filter 6, change this Filter mode to High Cut, as shown in Figure 8.10. Do this for each EQ Eight on each track.

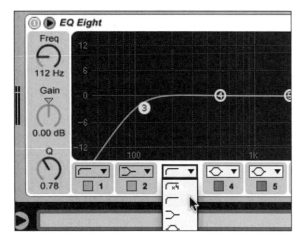

Figure 8.10 Change the Filter mode for an EQ Eight filter.
Source: Ableton AG

4. Now, go back into MIDI Mapping mode and select Filter 3 by clicking on it in EQ Eight. Map the Freq of Filter 3 to a knob on your controller that would be suitable for rapid EQ sweeps. After you've done this, click Filter 6 and do the same. Map Filter 6's Freq knob to a suitable knob on your MIDI controller, as shown in Figure 8.11. Do this for both tracks. Make sure you're mapping separate knobs, faders, or sliders to each of the Freq knobs.

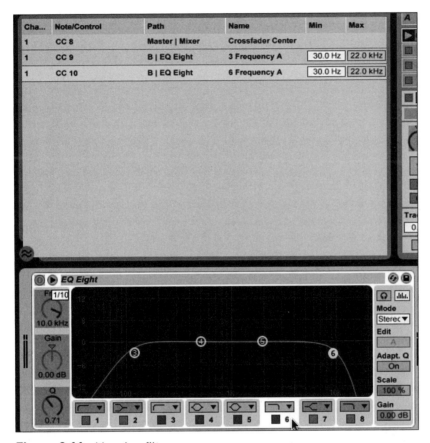

Figure 8.11 Mapping filters.
Source: Ableton AG

5. From here, you can easily add some sends and returns that have effects you'd like to use during your DJ performance. There's also the great possibility of recording your DJ performance in Session View over into the Arrangement View, as you did in an earlier chapter. This is a way to have some fun and then go back and refine your automation, and so on.

Live is an extremely powerful DJ tool. But as you can see, you want to spend a little time with it to get it ready for live DJ performance. I highly recommend setting up a template that you can use regularly if you're doing a lot of DJ gigs. Chapter 1 covered how to set up a template in the Default Song section. But, you can also just make an Ableton project that has all of your preferred DJ settings and save it. Then, when you need to start another DJ project, build from this project and save it as another name.

Now that we've spent some time with DJing, let's take a look at some suggestions for another important role in the musician community: the composer. We'll look at some valuable functionality in Ableton Live for composers.

Scoring Functions in Ableton Live

Live 9 has most of the options you'd expect when scoring for a movie. You can import movies and score along to them. There's also a wonderful marker system, known as *Locators*, that can be handy for remixing on the fly, live performances, and even when DJing. Let's examine Locators now.

NOTATION: While Live 9 may not include notation functionality, it does include MIDI functionality, including MIDI export. It is possible to export your MIDI parts, import them into another DAW, and then use the notation functionality of the other DAW to print out scores. Yes, this is an extra, annoying step. But if Live 9 speeds up your workflow in arranging and composing, you may not mind this step. Also, if you're scoring in another DAW but just need some of the Ableton functionality, it's possible to ReWire Ableton Live to the other DAW as a ReWire slave. Consult the Ableton manual on ReWire or take a look at my other book, *Using Rewire: Skill Pack* (Course Technology PTR, 2008).

---

1. Open the first music that we did together, or load a music project you've been working with on your own. In this project, locate a particular part of the song—for example, the chorus. Place the arrangement insert marker at the beginning of the chorus. To refresh your memory, the arrangement insert marker is the pulsing orange line. See Figure 8.12.

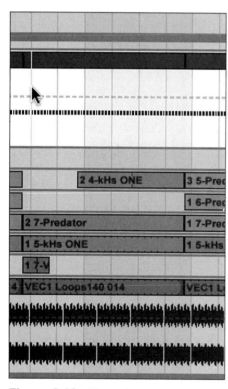

Figure 8.12 Place the arrangement insert marker in the Arrangement View.
Source: Ableton AG

2. When the arrangement insert marker is in place and pulsing, find the Locator Set button in the upper-right corner of the Arrangement window. By clicking the Set button, you can install a Locator that can be labeled and triggered for fast execution and quick information on when specific events occur in your performance. Click the button now and create a marker, as shown in Figure 8.13.

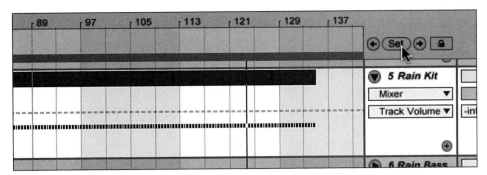

Figure 8.13 Place a Locator in the Arrangement View.
Source: Ableton AG

LOCATORS: Locators can be used only in the Arrangement View. There would be no place to put them in the Session View! Locators work very similarly to markers, as they are known in Pro Tools, Logic Pro, and so on, in the sense that they give you visual cues to identify where certain events begin and end in a song. But, they also have some other cool functionality for remixing and live performance, as you'll find out in this chapter.

3. Now that you've placed a Locator, let's name it. Select the Locator and then use the Command/Ctrl+R shortcut. Type in a name that fits the description, such as *Verse, Chorus 1, Chorus 2*, and so on. See Figure 8.14.

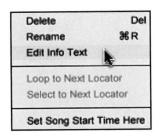

Figure 8.14 Label a Locator.
Source: Ableton AG

4. Now that a Locator is in place and labeled, you may want to include some more information about this section of the performance for other collaborators. If you right-click on the Locator you installed, you'll get an Edit Info Text option in the contextual menu. Select this option now, as shown in Figure 8.15.

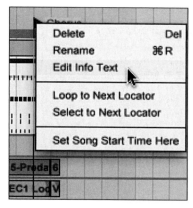

Figure 8.15 Set up a Locator for info text.
Source: Ableton AG

5. Once the Edit Info Text option is enabled, the Info View section of Ableton Live will either appear—or if it was already there, it will display a pulsing cursor that should prompt you to type something. Type any info about the event that the Locator is commemorating. See Figure 8.16. This could be something as simple as, "Guitar should start here, once recorded," or, "Cue the dancing girls."

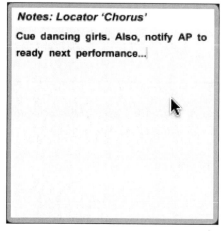

Figure 8.16 Info Text in the Info View section.
Source: Ableton AG

6. Place the arrangement insert marker at a different point of your project now. Once the section is located, click the Set button again to insert a new Locator. Label this Locator appropriately and press the spacebar to start up Ableton Live. Click on the first Locator that you placed and then try clicking the second Locator while Live is playing. Notice how you can trigger whole sections of a song to the beat within the Arrangement View, similar to the way you can trigger clips in the Session View. You can use the Quantization menu in the Transport section of Live's interface to adjust the quantization time of the cued Locators. For example, instead of having Live jump to the next Locator in one-bar increments, it could be adjusted to a half bar or a sixteenth note. See Figure 8.17.

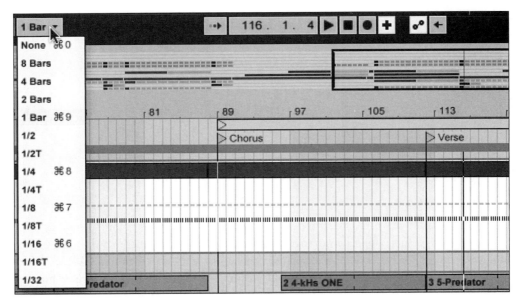

Figure 8.17 Adjusting the Quantization menu in the Arrangement View.
Source: Ableton AG

7. You can also use the Previous and Next Locator buttons, found on either side of the Set button, shown in Figure 8.18, to cycle or cue different markers during performance or when Live has stopped. Try the buttons now to get a feel for the way they work. By using these buttons, you've now become aware that there are a couple of ways to toggle different Locators into action. There's also another way—read on.

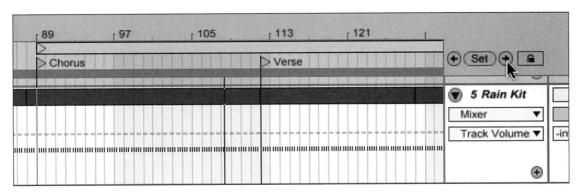

Figure 8.18 The Previous and Next Locator buttons and the Set button.
Source: Ableton AG

8. Another way to trigger Locators is by setting up MIDI keys or QWERTY buttons on a keyboard. This can be extremely cool for live performances, jam sessions, or even remixes. Try setting up a QWERTY key to be a trigger for a Locator. Click the Key button in the upper-right corner of Live, next to the MIDI button. See Figure 8.19. This enables Key Map mode.

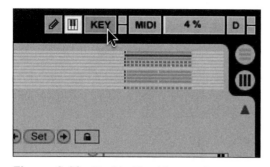

Figure 8.19 Enable Key Map mode.
Source: Ableton AG

9. Depending on your Ableton skin color, Key Map mode may appear in a different color. In my skin, different sections of my Ableton interface now appear as orange. Orange designates the functions that can be mapped. Click on a Locator while in Key Map mode. Once clicked, press a key on your computer QWERTY keyboard that you'd like to be mapped to this Locator. I'll use the Q button. See Figure 8.20. After you've mapped one key on your QWERTY keyboard, try mapping another. When you're finished mapping, click the Key button again to toggle out of Key Map mode.

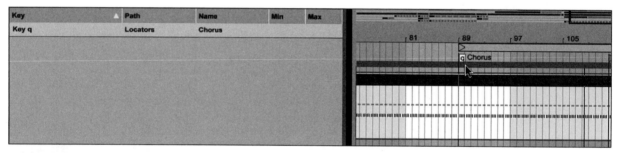

Figure 8.20 Mapping a Locator to a QWERTY key.
Source: Ableton AG

> **MIDI MAPPING LOCATORS:** To MIDI map Locators, click the MIDI button instead of the Key button. Select the Locator to which you would like to map and then press the MIDI controller key (or whatever you want to use on your controller) to map to.

Locators are incredibly powerful and offer some brilliant functionality for visual identification—and, as you can see, a way to move around rhythmically through your songs. I highly recommend spending some time with this powerful function of Ableton Live to see where it can benefit you in your work.

Another function needed for scoring movies, TV shows, and so on is the ability to bring video files into the project. Live accommodates this; let's try it out now.

Video in Ableton and Exporting Audio in Live 9

Before we begin, it's important to note that not just any video file will work. It needs to be in a format Apple QuickTime can read. Because QuickTime can export many different video file types, it might be a good idea to experiment before you spend a long time rendering an extremely long movie. Photo JPEG is reputed to be a good setting that is easy on the processor.

For the moment, let's add a movie file into Ableton, just to see how it's done. Do a search on your computer and see whether you can find a video (.mov, .mp4, and so on) file. Once you've located a file, proceed to the first step.

1. From an Explorer window, a Finder window, a Places location within the Ableton Browser, or iPhoto (which is what I'm using), drag a movie file onto an audio track in the Arrangement window of Ableton Live (see Figure 8.21). In the Arrangement View, the video will appear as audio. After the video is fully imported, the Video window, as it's known in Ableton, will appear, showing your video.

Figure 8.21 Drag a .mov into Live from iPhoto.
Source: Ableton AG

> **iPHOTO:** Keep in mind that just because a video is accepted in iPhoto, that doesn't necessarily mean it will work with Ableton Live. iPhoto supports a larger video file type range. But it never hurts to try, right?

2. Now that you've successfully brought the video into Ableton, let's talk about what you can do with it. Warping actually is possible, for those of you who just love to experiment. But it generally causes a lot of skipping and repeating audio. You can bring video into the Session View as well. However, the Video window will not appear in the Session View, and video will appear only as an audio clip. So, to sum it up, video works great in Ableton, but only in the Arrangement View.

   You can trim, cut, separate, and edit video exactly the way you edit audio clips in Ableton. Trimming is easy. Just move the cursor to the edge of the video, until the] or [appears. Once the cursor changes to one of these characters, just click and drag the corner of the clip. Instead of moving the clip, you're resizing. To separate the video clip into two videos, position the arrangement insert marker on the spot where you want the video to separate. Then, use the Command/Ctrl+E shortcut to force a separation. See Figure 8.22.

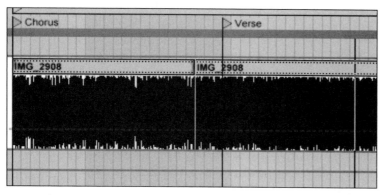

Figure 8.22 Separate a video clip in Ableton Live.
Source: Ableton AG

VIDEO AND SESSION VIEW: Even though you can't see video in the Session View, that doesn't mean the Session View isn't handy for video. Once the song is pieced together in Session View and you record the arrangement into Arrangement View, video will be there, waiting for you and playable. By placing a different video part on each section of the song, you've effectively created a rough cut of your video while arranging the song. Then you can fine-tune in Arrangement View.

---

3. You can export video (as well as audio) from Ableton. Pressing the Command/Ctrl+Shift+R shortcut will cause the Export Audio/Video screen to appear. Drag-select or highlight the beginning and ending of your arrangement that you want to render. Live works similarly to other DAWs in this regard. However, there are some wonderful nuances added to the Export Audio/Video menu. For example, you can export and have Ableton upload your song immediately to SoundCloud, a popular music-sharing service on the Internet. In the Session View, if you bring up the Export Audio/Video page, the top section will appear differently from if you'd brought up the Export Audio/Video page in the Arrangement View. As shown in Figure 8.23, the Session View version of Export Audio/Video has a Length section at the top. Here, you determine how long the scene or clip that is currently cued will be rendered. For example, if the scene is 8 bars long, you'll want to set the Length to 8 bars as well. Otherwise, you may get only 2 measures of an 8-bar part.

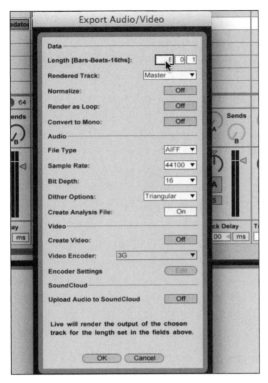

Figure 8.23 The Export Audio/Video page as it appears when triggered from the Session View.
Source: Ableton AG

Wrapping It Up

We've covered a lot of ground in Ableton Live 9 over the course of this book. You now know both views, you have keys and tips for mixing, song creation, and even sound design through the use of Instrument Racks, Drum Racks, and so on. You even know how to convert audio to MIDI and make songs by humming and beat-boxing. Really, you have a wealth of tools at your fingertips now, via the giant toolbox that is Ableton Live 9. Does this book cover everything? No, not by a long shot. It would take several books to cover every little thing Ableton Live 9 does. But what has been covered will give you the building blocks you need to successfully integrate Ableton Live 9 into your studio.

In closing, I highly recommend becoming a part of the Ableton community through Ableton.com's forums. People are constantly asking questions that you may want to know the answer to as well. I also highly recommend that you make a pact with yourself to do one project in only Ableton. That's what I did when I began learning it at version 3, and after a full album I was more than savvy. The Info View is always there in the lower-left corner as you go. Keep it on until it no longer gives you useful information.

Thanks so much for joining me on this guide through Ableton Live 9.

Index

Index

Index

Index